THE COMPLETE BALLOONING BOOK

THE COMPLETE BALLOONING BOOK

BY WILL HAYES

WORLD PUBLICATIONS

P.O. BOX 366
MOUNTAIN VIEW, CALIF. 94042

**Library of Congress Catalog Number
75-32444 ISBN 0-89037-111-3**

CONTENTS

TO BARBARA — — —

Thanks
    . . . . for letting me fly when the grass needed mowing;
    . . . . for letting me buy an inflator instead of replacing
           your worn-out refrigerator;
    . . . . for letting me go to Europe to balloon with friends
           instead of to Nebraska to visit your relatives . . . .

WITH LOVE AND APPRECIATION

FOREWORD

The Complete Ballooning Book tells how and why balloons fly, how you can earn a balloon pilot's license, where you can buy a balloon and how the whole ballooning movement started and grew. Before you read on, however, allow me to inject a word of caution. The story of ballooning is a siren's song that says, "Come fly with me!" Few can resist the temptation.

Ballooning is the oldest and newest of man's attempts to conquer the skies. Almost 200 years have passed since the Montgolfiers observed rising smoke and saw this as a means of flight. Today, new technology provides the fabrics and burner systems that make modern ballooning what it is. During these 200 years, a century was wasted when man turned away from balloons to give his attention to other forms of flight. But now balloons are back. The question is, why?

Maybe it's because they're so colorful, or that they're (at times) quiet, or that they're such an anachronism. Maybe it's because they tend to bring forth the best qualities of mankind: sharing . . . . laughter . . . . cooperation . . . . joy . . . . inventiveness . . . . . peace. Perhaps it's the delight in the eyes of a child when he touches a balloon, or the flights of fancy that inspire youngsters and oldsters alike, or the hours when the balloonist is alone aloft and feels the mystique of being one with God.

In what other aircraft is your flight route so unimportant? What other form of flight allows you to become part of the wind? How else can you be suspended quietly and gently just above the tree tops.

The Complete Ballooning Book has been fun to write, but whatever errors or omissions you find were probably due to my frustration of having to write when I wanted to fly. But for those parts that delight and inform you, send your kudos along to fellow aeronauts Ted Farrell, Dr. Clayton Thomas, Matt Wiederkehr, Bruce Comstock, Mark Semich, Bobby Sparks, Dan Hacker, Portis Wolley, Dee Sloan, and a host of concerned associates in the Federal Aviation Administration. Neither the manuscript nor I would have gotten off the ground without their encouragement and help.

To those countless others who shared their ballooning aspirations with me and are generous enough to forgive me if I do not separately call their names, special thanks.

Ballooning has grown at a geometric rate in the past few years. There are more than 1,000 balloons filling the skies of the United States, and four times as many pilots. These numbers will multiply in the years ahead and it is my hope that you will be among them. If you are, I wish you only blue skies . . . warm, gentle breezes . . . and soft landings.

Dr. Will Hayes
Santa Barbara, California

HISTORY OF BALLOONING
1

The history of ballooning is the early history of aviation itself. By 1783, when Joseph and Etienne Montgolfier built the hot air balloon that finally allowed men to shrug his earthly bonds, the theory behind balloon flight was many centuries old. The ancient Greek mathematician Archimedes had discovered that light objects placed in a liquid or in the air would be buoyed upward with a force equal to the weight displaced by the object.

One of the first flying machines based on this concept was hypothesized by an Italian priest named Francesco de Lana-Terzi. By exhausting all the air from four huge copper globes, de Lana reasoned that he could make the globes buoyant enough to raise his airship aloft.

While the theory behind de Lana's craft was sound, the technology available to him condemned the project to failure. At that time it was impossible to construct spheres light enough to buoy even themselves when exhausted of air. They were not strong enough to avoid collapse as the internal air was pumped away.

Powered heavier-than-air flight was forced to wait until technology advanced enough to provide a light and efficient powerplant. In a like manner it would take a technological advance to trigger lighter-than-air flight. It would require a lighter balloon apparatus and the discovery of gas that was lighter in relation to the atmosphere than a mere vacuum.

The gas was discovered in 1766 by the Englishman Henry Cavendish. He called it "phlogiston," while others called it "inflammable air." Twenty years after its discovery, Pilatre de Rozier, the first man to go aloft in a balloon, often entertained audiences using this "inflammable air." The gas is known today as hydrogen, and its inflammable nature has caused more than a few aerial tragedies.

In 1774 the English physicist Joseph Priestly discovered "dephlogisticated air" (oxygen) and published *Experiments and Observations on Different Kinds of Air*. Two years later a translation of Priestly's treatise was published in France.

One interested reader of *Experiments and Observations* was an affluent French papermaker named Joseph Montgolfier. He began speculating about flight during the early 1780s. Within a short time his younger brother Etienne also grew excited about flight and became deeply involved in the experiments.

The brothers Montgolfier tried paper and linen bags filled with phlogiston, but these materials were much too porous to capture a gas only one-thirteenth as dense as the atmosphere. These experiments were abandoned in the hope that some other kind of rarified air could be discovered.

The Montgolfiers soon discovered that smoke provided this rarified air (much later it was determined that heated air, not smoke, provided the lift for their balloons). How Joseph and Etienne Montgolfier discovered this lifting power has become a matter of considerable speculation among historians, and three stories have been advanced.

Some believe that the brothers watched small bits of burned paper rise up in the flames of a fireplace. A second story involves a chemise which had been put by the fire to dry. Supposedly heat radiating from the fire warmed air inside the skirt, causing it to float aloft. A third account claims that Madame Montgolfier threw a paper bag into the fire at such an angle that it filled with smoke before touching the flames and floated safely up the flue.

Whatever the cause, Joseph and Etienne Montgolfier were soon filling small paper bags with smoke and watching them drift up and away. Concluding that smoke had some magic property, the brothers began experimenting with different types of smoke. They tried wood, waste paper; even old disgarded shoes and rotten meat. Apparently they felt that the more noxious the smoke the better its lifting power. Eventually the pair settled on a combination of straw and wool.

The Montgolfiers constructed gradually larger balloon bags and achieved more significant flights. Their first small linen bag reached an altitude of 70 feet, while a second and larger envelope flew to a height of 600 feet. A third balloon had a diameter of 35 feet and soared to 1000 feet. Another large balloon reached an altitude of more than a mile and floated more than a mile from its launching point.

Joseph Montgolfier was convinced early in his experiments that balloons could be very useful in war, and France was often at war. In the early 1780s the enemy was England, and Montgolfier proposed a plan to transport soldiers, by balloon, over the walls of Britain's impregnable fortress at Gibraltar. While this notion was never carried out, it was a preview of 170 years of military ballooning.

As the Montgolfier balloons grew larger, they developed more lift. The balloon that reached 6000 feet was capable of lifting an additional 400 to 500 pounds of payload. The time was ripe for passengers to be carried aloft.

On September 18, 1783 the Montgolfiers sent aloft from Paris a hot air balloon with a duck, a rooster and a sheep on board. The balloon was 57 feet high and 41 feet in diameter. Louis XVI and Marie Antionette witnessed the flight, and Louis was sufficiently impressed to decree that the three animals would live out their years in the luxury of his Royal Menagerie.

Since no ill effects were noticed on the animals, manned flight was the next step. Initially, the King of France wanted to send a criminal aloft. Louis feared the dangers of manned flight and reasoned that a criminal would not be especially missed if he fell victim to some aerial mishap.

A young French chemist named Francoise Pilatre de Rozier was scandalized that the glory for man's conquest of the air should fall to a common fellon. He convinced the Marquis d'Arlandes that they should have the honor and the Marquis began to press at court for this privilege. He finally convinced Marie Antionette, who supposedly exercised her feminine charm to change Louis' mind.

The Montgolfiers built a much larger balloon of linen coated with paper. During the Autumn of 1783, Pilatre de Rozier made several tethered ascents to learn how much straw and wool should be burned to produce varying durations of flight. Gradually he became quite skilled at burning the correct amounts of fuel and by November the Montgolfiers were ready to launch.

On November 21, 1783 a huge crowd gathered to watch de Rozier and the Marquis d'Arlandes make history's first manned free flight. The crowd—which included King Louis XVI, Marie Antoinette, the royal court of Versailles and half the city of Paris—was estimated at over 400,000, easily the largest gathering of people at any place in the world up until that time.

Just before 2:00 p.m. the daring pair of aeronauts floated aloft to a great cheer, and sailed slowly over Paris for about 25 minutes. The balloon carried the Marquis and de Rozier only about five miles, but manned aviation had finally gotten off the ground.

Only 10 days after this hot air balloon (they were henceforth called *Montgolfiers*) was flown, another Frenchman, Jacques Charles, launched the first gas-filled passenger balloon. (They were thereafter called *Charlieres*). It contained hydrogen and carried two passengers for a flight of much longer duration than the *Montgolfiers*. Soon hydrogen balloons were airborn all over France, and *Charlieres* quickly replaced the rather clumsy and inefficient *Montgolfiers*.

Charles had been experimenting with hydrogen-filled balloons throughout 1783. He overcame the problem of porous cloth and paper by coating silk with a light film of rubber. His first balloon was a sphere 12 feet in diameter and it weighed 25 pounds. Although this was rather small in comparison with

later efforts, hydrogen gas production was not well refined and filling a balloon meant three days of work.

In 1783 hydrogen gas was generated by the action of sulfuric acid on iron filings. Charles' generator was so leaky that he needed nearly 500 pounds of acid and 1000 pounds of iron to fill his balloon. But the balloon was inflated finally and transported to the Champ de Mars, then a large cleared area and currently the site of the Eiffel Tower.

On August 27th, the *Globe* was launched. It quickly ascended into a rain cloud at about 3000 feet and disappeared from sight. About 45 minutes later it descended in the town of Gonesse about 15 miles from Paris. Terrified villagers attacked the balloon bag with pitchforks, scythes and hoes, ripping it to shreds and thus protecting their wives and children from the supernatural monster that had descended on their town.

After the success of his first balloon flight, Charles designed and constructed a larger hydrogen balloon. Through sheer genius he hit precisely on a design that still serves modern balloon aeronauts. It looked like a peeled orange 27½ feet in diameter. Alternately colored red and yellow panels were tapered from top to bottom to form the balloon's gores. The end effect was that the balloon looked like it had the characteristic segments of an orange.

A basket was suspended from the balloon bag by cables attached to a netting that evenly distributed the payload weight over the balloon's upper surface. The neck of the balloon was open to allow expanding gas to escape as the aerostat gained altitude. Charles even provided a valve at the top of the balloon to allow gas to be valved off when a descent was desired. Ballast carried in the wicker basket provided upward control.

On December 1, 1783, Charles and Aine Robert ascended from the Tuileries gardens in Paris. When compared to the clumsy *Montgolfiers,* the smaller *Charliere* ascended with perilous speed. The collected multitudes gasped, but the aeronauts were in complete control of their craft. For two hours Charles and Robert floated above the gradually changing landscape, finally landing 27 miles from Paris near the village of Nesles.

Within the next year several significant aerial milestones were passed. On January 10, 1784, the first giant balloon was launched. *Le Flessile* was 131 feet high and 104 feet in diameter. In February an initial ascent was made in Italy and in May Mme. Thible of Lyons made the first free ascent by a woman. By August balloon fever had spread to England.

Inventors in France, Italy, England and Germany were building and flying balloons. Many of these attempts ended in failure. In contrast, however, Jean-Pierre Blanchard's experiments were eminently successful.

Blanchard was a French aeronaut. On January 7, 1785, with the financial backing and participation of Dr. John Jeffries, an American physicist living in England, he made what became a classic and historic balloon flight. Blanchard and Jeffries departed Dover on a strong wind that was expected to take them across the English Channel. The flight was quite rough, with the balloon alternately shooting up and descending rapidly almost to the top of the waves. By the time they sighted the shores of France, Blanchard and Jeffries had jettisoned everything, even their trousers. When they landed their gas balloon at Calias the daring pair became instant heroes, the first to cross the Channel. A monument marks the landing spot and the balloon basket is still on exhibit at the Calias museum.

Eight years later Jean-Pierre Blanchard sailed to America and made many balloon ascents. At Philadelphia in 1783, one of his flights was observed by President George Washington. Blanchard landed 15 miles away in Woodbury, New Jersey. He returned to Philadelphia that evening and visited Washington in the Executive mansion. He presented the President with a small American flag that he had carried aloft. In return, Washington accorded him the first official Presidential honor paid to a sky explorer, a custom restored for returning astronauts

Despite his historic English Channel crossing, Blanchard is best remembered in America for a balloon flight during the late 1780s. As an experiment, he parachuted a dog to earth, accomplishing the first parachute drop in the New World. Spectators at the landing site observed that the dog reached earth safely, but it was too frightened to even bark!

In all, Blanchard made 60 successful ascents. During his last flight in 1808, he suffered a heart attack in mid-air and barely survived the crash after he lost control of his balloon. He died about a year later, but Blanchard was not the first victim of man's aerial adventures.

On June 15, 1785, Francoise Pilatre de Rozier—the first balloon aeronaut—attempted to fly a balloon from France to England. In the process he became the first ballooning casualty. His mistake was attempting to combine the features of both hot air and gas balloons, reasoning that a gas balloon would provide constant lift, while a hot air bag mounted below would allow for better vertical control. Unfortunately, de Rozier did not take into account the highly combustible nature of hydrogen gas.

Shortly after liftoff, the gas bag exploded and the balloon's two occupants plummetted to earth from an altitude of about 500 meters. Pilatre was killed instantly on impact and his co-pilot died shortly after. A third victim was de Rozier's fiance, who died of grief and shock upon seeing her beloved's violent end.

Within a decade after the first manned flight, balloon fever had swept Europe. Studies were being made of the upper atmosphere. Pleasure voyages grew common, and there were daring exhibitions of aerial acrobatics and stunts. Balloons became larger and more elaborate. One—

Le Giant—provided its passengers with a wicker house measuring nearly 20 feet in height and 15 feet in width. Balloon flights were the rage of Europe.

Among those in Paris who became interested in the new science was the American envoy to France, Benjamin Franklin. A statesman and scientist of repute, Franklin had made numerous experiments with kites. A skeptic reputedly asked him, "Of what use is a balloon?" Franklin rhetorically replied, "Of what use is a new born babe?"

Distance flights caught the fancy of ballooning enthusiasts at the beginning of the 19th Century. Charles Green, England's greatest early balloonist, made the first notable cross-country flight in November of 1836. Ascending from London with two passengers in a hydrogen-filled balloon, he flew 480 miles in 18 hours, finally coming to earth in the Duchy of Nassau, Germany.

By the middle of the 19th Century, balloonists were talking seriously about flying the Atlantic Ocean. John Wise, an American balloonist from Philadelphia, constructed a balloon for his projected crossing. On July 1, 1859, he took three passengers on a test flight from St. Louis, Missouri. During the almost 21 hours aloft in the *Atlantic,* the crew experienced possibly the worst weather ever reported by aeronauts.

The *Atlantic* was well-designed as an over-water balloon. It had two "cars" mounted one above the other, with the bottom car designed as a life boat. (More than a century later this same arrangement was used for modern Atlantic attempts.)

The early part of the journey was uneventful, and the steady southwest wind moved the balloon along the 5000-foot level at a brisk speed. The aeronauts' account of the beauty and serenity of Lake Erie, Lake Ontario and Niagara Falls shows they had no clue of the impending gale moving in behind them.

Suddenly the wind hit. The car lurched and plummeted toward the towering waves of Lake Ontario below. It struck the water head on, and with the erratic behavior characteristic of balloons, bounced back into the sky. Time after time the aerostat dropped and rose again.

The lake shore raced toward them with frightening speed. Over went the grapnel, but the speed and inertia of the balloon broke off its hooks as it hit the trees. Through brush and trees the balloon raced until it was finally dashed to earth. In its headlong rush to a final resting place, the balloon had scoured a wide swath of broken trees and uprooted bushes. Miraculously, no one was injured, and a new distance record of 803 miles had been set.

Wise patched the *Atlantic* and searched for another backer, but before he was ready to finally attempt his trans-oceanic flight the Civil War erupted. After the war he again sought financial backing, finding it at last with the New York *Daily Graphic*. Unfortunately, the publishers hurried his flight. The huge 400,000 cubic-foot balloon that he had constructed ruptured near the top and spilled its precious hydrogen gas. The balloon was repaired and Wise finally pushed off toward Europe. He made only 40 miles before being forced to abandon his trip.

Balloonists also became interested in high altitude flights, and an Englishman named Henry Coxwell emerged as the foremost altitude pilot. James Glaishen, director of the meteorology department of Greenwich Observatory, commissioned Coxwell to carry him aloft for high-altitude scientific observations. On September 5, 1862, they ascended to an altitude of more than seven miles over Wolverhampton, England. Seeking only to reach a moderately high altitude for the scientific experiments, the pair inadvertently became the first men to probe the stratosphere. Without oxygen breathing equipment on the flight, they risked their lives by exposure to the cold and the danger of hypoxia.

During the second hour of the flight—above 15,000 feet—they were breathing with great difficulty in the cold, rarified air. As the balloon continued to ascend, Coxwell began making preparations for the descent. To his horror, he discovered the deflation valve rope hanging outside the basket just beyond his reach. He struggled for it several times, but was unsuccessful.

Glaishen was already unconscious and Coxwell knew he was fading fast. If he couldn't grasp and pull the release valve rope, they would surely die.

In the bitter cold and stillness of the rarified upper atmosphere, Coxwell desperately leaned out as far as he dared, finally managing to grip the rope. He tugged on it as fiercely as his waning strength would permit, and the soft hissing above whispered that he had finally succeeded. The valve was open and the balloon began to descend. Coxwell could not rejoice however. He had finally "blacked out."

When the men eventually regained consciousness and slowed the balloon's overly fast descent, Coxwell and Glaishen read the barometer and discovered they had reached an altitude of 39,000 feet. Their ascent—made without oxygen, with a minimum of protective clothing, and with virtually no knowledge of the upper atmosphere—ranks among the greatest of aeronautical feats. The altitude record they set in their open-basket balloon stood for more than a century.

The American Civil War marked the first extensive use of balloons for military purposes. Although the French had made reconnaissance flights and even tried dropping bombs by remote control as early as June of 1794, America's Thaddeus Lowe pioneered the use of balloons for military purposes. Lowe was born in New Hampshire in 1832, and at 12 ran off with a showman who had come to town with a magic act. This was only the first chapter to a life filled with adventure.

By 1858, Lowe had behind him nearly a decade of experimenting with hydrogen and various balloon designs. He began constructing the *City of New York,* a huge 725,000 cubic-foot gas balloon that he hoped to pilot across the Atlantic Ocean. "Professor" Lowe's launch site was to be Philadelphia, but a series of delays ended in disaster when heavy winds destroyed the gas bag. Nonplussed, Lowe began preparations for a continental flight to begin at Cincinnati.

By this time, April of 1861, the Civil War began. On April 20th, Lowe ascended on what was to become an unexpected adventure. At sunrise he was 18,000 feet over the Allegheny Mountains. Without charts or maps, he was unaware of his position, and when evening fell he began to descend, landing in North Carolina. As soon as he told the rapidly growing crowd that he was from the North, he was placed under arrest and taken to Unionville. There he learned that he was, in fact, the first Yankee to be captured during the War Between the States.

Lowe was soon released and went to Washington to meet with President Lincoln and offer his services as head of a Balloon Corps. His proposal was accepted and on June 18, 1861, Lowe dictated the first telegraphic message from a balloon. By the time Lowe reached ground, Lincoln had returned his message with hearty congratulations.

By November of 1861, Thaddeus Lowe had forged a highly efficient Aeronautic Corps to operate with McClellan's Army of the Potomac. Among his aerial armada were the *Union* and *Intrepid*—each 32,000 cubic feet—and three smaller aerostats, the *Constitution,* the *United States,* and the *Washington.* The "spy in the sky" was born.

Lowe's balloons flew on tethers high above enemy lines while observers used telegraph equipment to relay messages to the troops below. Occasionally a tether line would part and the free balloon became a target for gunners on both sides. The obvious advantage of seeing the field of battle laid out below like a chess board made Lowe's Corps of considerable value to the Union Army. As an example, Major General A.W. Greeley, Chief Signal Officer of the Army, reported after one battle that "Lowe's quick thinking was the horseshoe nail that saved an army."

Following the war, Lowe opened an Aeronautic Amphitheater in New York, where he sold rides and performed various balloon stunts. He is also remembered as being among the first balloonists to use coal gas instead of hydrogen in a balloon.

Although completely overshadowed by Lowe's exploits, the Confederacy also had a balloon corps. Captain John Randolph Bryan, a cavalryman from Virginia, was the pilot of the Confederate States' one-balloon air armada. Bryan flew a cotton balloon powered by hot air and managed to make several crucial observations before losing his balloon.

A little later another Confederate balloon was observed, an aerostat that caused considerable hilarity among Union troops. Starved for raw materials, the Confederacy was forced to use silk dresses donated by Southern ladies to construct the balloon envelope. Needless to say, this resulted in a somewhat colorful balloon. The patchwork balloon was captured on July 4, 1863, and taken to Washington where it was cut into pieces for souvenirs. Thus ended the air force of the Confederate States of America.

A decade later, the Franco-Prussian War provided the next showcase for military balloons. The Prussians quickly struck toward Paris, surrounded the French capitol and put the city under siege. There were too few Prussian troops, however, to conquer the French provinces and maintain the seige on Paris.

Between September 1870 and January of 1871, 62 balloons were launched from Paris to maintain contact with the provinces and the outside world. Six of these balloons were captured and two others blew out to sea, but more than 100 Parisians escaped the siege.

The balloons also served as vehicles for the first airmail delivery. Approximately 2,500,000 letters were delivered in this fashion, and covers from these letters are highly prized among modern stamp collectors.

Toward the end of the 19th Century, European and North American scientists became very interested in Arctic exploration. The romantic ideal was to become the first to set foot on the North Pole, and many attempts were launched by sea and over the polar ice cap.

Saloman August Andree, a Swedish scientist, hit upon the idea of taking a balloon flight as the quickest and easiest way to reach the pole. In 1876 the 22-year-old Andree had visited Philadelphia to participate in the International Exhibition. There he met the crusty old balloon adventurer, John Wise.

Wise had finally abandoned hope of personally crossing the Atlantic in a balloon, but he was still convinced that the feat could be accomplished. Andree was soon enflamed with this same belief, and by 1890 he was planning a balloon flight over the North Pole.

A giant gas balloon—christened *Ornen* (the *Eagle*)—was built. It contained a sleeping area, numerous scientific instruments and provisions for a month's flight. Between the car and the balloon was a compartment that held sleds, a folding canoe, guns and ammunition, and provisions for four months. These were safeguards against the possibility of being forced to return across the ice.

Ornen incorporated an innovation that allowed the balloon to be sailed and steered. Normally a balloon floats along at almost the same speed as the wind, making the use of a sail impractical. But as soon as a balloon can be slowed in relation to the wind, it can be maneuvered by means of sails attached to the envelope.

Andree equipped *Ornen* with three trail ropes, each 1000 meters in length. The three ropes weighed a total of 750 kilograms, and when dragged through the sea or across ice they effectively slowed the balloon. *Ornen* carried three square sails to help steer the balloon.

Foreseeing a possible buildup of snow on top of the balloon, Andree provided *Ornen* with a slick cap over the top of the balloon. A layer of silk was varnished and polished, making the surface slick enough that snow accumulations would build only to a low level before sliding harmlessly off.

Ornen was inflated and lay in readiness in a large balloon shelter at Dane Island during June of 1896. Andree intended to launch from Dane Island, the northwestern tip of Spitzbergen, as soon as the required southerly wind arrived. He and his two fellow explorers waited . . . and waited. They waited an entire frustrating summer, being unable to launch. Finally they packed up and sailed back to Stockholm.

Over the winter of 1896 and 1897, Andree continued making modifications on his balloon. The most important of these was to enlarge the balloon envelope. The entire balloon had proved heavier than expected once constructed, and Andree desired to improve its lifting capacity.

In late May of 1897, Andree's expedition again arrived at Dane Island where they inflated *Ornen* inside its hangar and settled in to wait for a southerly wind. For nearly six weeks they waited, a period during which the wind was either completely missing or blowing from all but the required direction. Finally it blew from the south and Andree decided to launch.

The hangar's removable north wall was quickly knocked away and the balloon was cut loose from its moorings. It was an ill-omened launch from the very start. Two of the three trail ropes were inadvertently left behind and the balloon experienced difficulty in gaining altitude. The launch crew noted that the car even splashed briefly into the sea just offshore.

Andree, with his companions Knut Fraenkel and Nils Strindberg, left Dane Island on July 11, 1897. The balloon was expected to stay aloft for 30 days, but the flight ended abruptly at 7:00 a.m. only three days later, when the balloon disappeared. Only diary accounts and exposed film eventually revealed the balloon's fate.

When the balloon had plunged into the sea upon launch, Andree was forced to jettison 200 kilograms of sand ballast to achieve a suitable altitude. The balloon apparently still lacked lift. Too much ballast was jettisoned, however, and the balloon shot up to nearly 2000 meters, far above the planned 80 to 100 meters altitude foreseen in Andree's flight plan.

At this altitude the one remaining trail rope would not reach the water or ice and *Ornen* was left purely at the whim of the wind. Since the balloon was still headed north, Andree decided to do nothing for a time, but soon *Ornen* was being blown east and then even south. A decision was made to vent some gas and descend to a lower altitude, where the balloon stood a better chance of being maneuvered.

A gas valve was opened and the balloon descended, but the valve became stuck open and gas continued to escape at a slow, but fatal speed. This lost lift was further complicated by ice forming on the lines of the balloon. Andree had foreseen snow accumulations on the balloon bag but he had not considered ice freezing to other surfaces.

A cold arctic fog eventually proved to be the downfall of *Ornen.* The heavy mist turned to ice on the balloon and altitude was gradually lost. Andree and his crew jettisoned all unnecessary items inside their gondola, but they were only briefly postponing the inevitable. Increasing ice and the steady gas loss were taking their toll.

After flying for 65 hours, *Ornen* was forced down. It crashed to the ice, 300 miles from its starting point at 81'15" north latitude and 29'52" east longitude, still 500 miles from the pole. The explorers had covered more than 500 miles, but much of the distance had been at the mercy of shifting winds.

To avoid dying of cold, Andree and his companions were

forced to reach solid ground before winter arrived. They set off toward the east with their sledges, folding canoe and supplies. The return journey was a nightmare, and the route was constantly altered as sea currents and shifting winds moved the ice flows. Even on good days, the group was able to make only two or three miles over the ice and around long open stretches of water. Tragically, much of this distance was wiped out each day by the gradual westward drift of the ice.

The one saving grace of Andree's struggle was that food was plentiful and they did not need to cut into their precious reserve stores. Polar bears abounded and were easy to kill. The party subsisted quite well on the flesh and body fat of the bears they regularly shot.

After four months of heroic struggle, Andree and his companions reached White Island at the northern end of Spitsbergen. There they made a hasty camp and settled in for the winter. The last journal entry was dated October 17, 1897.

For 33 years the fate of Andree's expedition was a mystery. Three messages—one by carrier pigeon and two contained in buoys—were discovered within a year, but all three were written before *Ornen* crashed. Finally in August of 1930, Norwegian seal hunters discovered the remains of the explorers' bodies, the log books and the film. The remains were sent to Stockholm and honored with a state funeral, and a special ship was dispatched to bring home the remainder of Andree's camp.

For several years the cause of Andree's death was widely speculated. When found, the dead explorers still had more than enough supplies to last the winter, and the area abounded with seals and polar bears. They had plenty of fuel, and one of their stoves was found full of fuel and even in operating condition. Under these circumstances, there appeared to be no reason for the explorers to die.

Cold was hypothesized, as was death from carbon monoxide poisoning. The latter hypothesis was widely accepted, because the danger of operating a primus stove in an enclosed area was well known. Several years passed before the true cause of death was established.

Upon closely examining the explorers' diaries, a young Swedish physician began to suspect that the men had died of trichinosis. Andree and his companions had complained of open sores, joint pains and other symptoms of the disease during their struggle over the ice. The physician was fortunate enough to examine the remains of a bear that the explorers had shot, and the mystery was solved. Under microscopic examination, the bear was clearly infected with the disease.

Three years after Andree began his ill-fated adventure, an event occurred in Germany that virtually spelled the end for balloons. Since the first manned flight, many experiments had been attempted to make balloons steerable—everything from oars to propellers had been unsuccessful. Only Andree's drag lines and sails provided limited maneuverability.

With the advent of a lightweight and powerful gasoline engine, however, Count Ferdinand von Zeppelin hit on the correct solution to a steerable lighter-than-air craft. He streamlined a balloon, fitted it with one of the new engines and on July 1, 1900 flew the first completely dirigible aircraft. Man could now turn his aerial machines and even fly into the wind!

Prior to von Zeppelin's efforts, a number of inventors had turned their attentions to developing navigable balloons, but all were defeated by the lack of a suitable power plant. As early as 1783, a young French military engineer named Jean Baptiste Meusnier presented what can best be described as a prophetic design for a dirigible balloon.

Meusnier's design was an eliptical balloon in the shape of a football or rugby ball approximately 260 feet long. Below the huge balloon was suspended an open carriage in the form of a boat. Propellers were attached amidship, and a rudder was provided. Only the lack of a suitable powerplant prevented the fruition of Meusnier's dirigible design.

A bit later two Swiss inventors, John Pauly and Durs Egg, attempted to build a dirigible. It was shaped somewhat like a dolphin and incorporated a "ballonet" (an invention of Meusnier's consisting of a rigid inner balloon to give the dirigible shape) and a sliding sandbox weight to help trim the craft fore and aft. The Pauly-Egg design never flew, but the ballonet achieved a degree of fame. The great American showman P.T. Barnum acquired the small balloon and used it in ascents by his noted midget, General Tom Thumb.

Additional strides were made by a French clockmaker, Pierre Jullien, in 1850. Jullien constructed a streamlined lighter-than-air craft model and flew it quite successfully inside a large auditorium. The model incorporated many features found in later successful dirigibles. Jullien stiffened his model with a light wire frame and placed the gondola up under the front part of the model. He also used two outboard propellers driven by small clock springs. Jullien later developed a full-sized version of his small scale model, but he was also defeated by the lack of a suitable motor.

Henri Giffard in 1852 flew the first powered and navigable balloon. His craft was 144 feet long and sharply pointed at both ends. He powered it with a light steam engine capable of moving the craft at a rate of 6 miles per hour. Elaborate precautions were taken to keep the firebox isolated from the explosive hydrogen contained in the envelope.

Giffard actually flew 17 miles on his first attempt, and on other occasions was able to fly complete circles to demonstrate the maneuverability of his aircraft. Unfortunately, Giffard was also handicapped by the lack of a sufficiently powerful (and yet light) engine. His dirigible's top speed of six miles per hour made it effective in only dead calm air. With anything more than a gentle breeze it was as ineffective and vulnerable as a free balloon.

During the late 1870s an American, Charles F. Ritchel, developed a workable human-powered dirigible. The first powered aircraft to fly in America consisted of a 25-foot-long sausage-shaped envelope with a sort of bicycle frame suspended below it. By pedaling hard a small propeller could be driven, thus moving the machine through the air. Directional flight was achieved by angling the propeller in different directions. Even with a small and wiry pilot, Ritchel's little dirigible could develop a top speed of only 3½ m.p.h.

Paul Haenlein displayed the first dirigible using an internal combustion engine late in 1872. Haenlein built his craft in Vienna, and despite the fact it was never flown free, the dirigible achieved an estimated speed of 9 m.p.h. travelling in still air.

Two French army engineers flew the next notable dirigible in August of 1884. It was 165 feet long and had a long narrow car hung below the "sausage." The Renard-Krebs aircraft was powered by an electrical engine, contained a slide weight for trimming, and had efficient control surfaces for both horizontal and vertical direction changes.

Renard and Krebs launched *La France* on seven successful flights and were able to achieve a top speed of nearly 15 m.p.h. *La France* was so maneuverable it could accomplish a 180-degree turn with a radius of only 160 yards. But this dirigible was also limited by its powerplant. The battery capacity severely shortened its range of operation.

Karl Woelfert, a German doctor, flew several successful models of gasoline-powered dirigibles, but the engine he used caused his hydrogen balloon to explode on a test flight. Woelfert and his co-pilot perished.

By the end of the 19th Century, aluminum became available, and light internal frames could be constructed for lighter-than-air ships. Von Zeppelin developed his rigid aircraft at the turn of the century. His first huge ship, 420 feet in length, flew successfully on July 2, 1900. Within nine years his airships were making flights covering 600 miles in two days.

By 1910 von Zeppelin's dirigibles were regularly engaged in the first commercial airline business. The zeppelins could climb to 20,000 feet and achieve speeds of 70 m.p.h. Their range was sufficient for Germany to mount bombing raids on England during World War I.

Without suitable bombsights, the German zeppelin pilots used an ingenious method of spotting the target. An observer would be winched down several thousand feet below the zeppelins in a streamlined gondola. With the zeppelin high in the clouds and the gondola below, the observer could guide the mother craft over a target and order down the bombs at the correct moment.

After the war, two pilots of fixed-wing aircraft became the first to conquer the Atlantic Ocean, but the lure of transoceanic flight in lighter-than-air craft was still there. Flying an English duplication of one of Count von Zeppelin's wartime raiders called R-34, Major G.H. Scott and his crew crossed the Atlantic in July of 1919. The R-34 landed on Long Island 100 hours after take-off. Due to storms during the crossing, the aircraft had only a half hour of fuel remaining when it landed.

After World War I, the Zeppelin manufacturing works swung back into production, and dirigible manufacture was begun in the United States. The noted German dirigible *Graf Zeppelin* logged nearly 600 commercial flights (140 across the Atlantic) and 1,000,000 miles of service without accidents. Other dirigibles were not so lucky.

The *Shenandoah*, first American-built dirigible and first to use inert helium in place of explosive hydrogen, crashed during a violent electrical storm in Ohio. Thirteen crew members were killed when the hull, longer than two football fields, was ripped into three parts by the force of the storm.

One final dirigible disaster sounded the death knell for rigid lighter-than-air vehicles—the burning of the *Hindenburg.* Nazi Germany looked to the *Hindenburg* as a symbol of national pride. Festooned with swastikas, it could cross the Atlantic between Germany and the United States in two days, an incredible speed when compared with the week a luxury ocean liner took to make the same crossing.

The *Hindenburg* was 803 feet in length and carried more than seven million cubic feet of gas. Its four huge Mercedes engines, developing 1100 horse power, could push the dirigible along at a cruising speed of nearly 80 m.p.h. On May 6, 1936 *Hindenburg* began regular air service, with a $400 price tag for each ticket.

Luxury was the rule aboard the *Hindenburg.* Only the finest accommodations and food were provided for each guest, and the view of the Atlantic was unexcelled. Occasionally passengers were even treated to a view of huge icebergs floating across the North Atlantic.

Despite its opulence and the strength of its construction, *Hindenburg* had one fatal flaw. Highly inflammable hydrogen gas provided its lift. This particular flaw had not gone entirely unnoticed by German engineers, but inert helium gas was available in sufficient quantities (and at great expense) only in the United States. With diplomatic relations strained between the United States and Nazi Germany, an embargo was placed on the export of helium. As a result, *Hindenburg* was forced to spend its first year of service using hydrogen.

Elaborate precautions were taken to prevent ignition of the hydrogen gas. Smoking was allowed only in a specially-designed

Luxury was the rule aboard the *Hindenburg. . .*

and pressurized room, and the *Hindenburg* steward in charge of that room was the only person on board with matches. The kitchen was similarly safeguarded, and aluminum was used extensively (even in the lounge piano) for both its lack of weight and its resistance to static electricity buildup.

Despite all precautions, the *Hindenburg* caught fire and was destroyed while landing at Lakehurst, New Jersey. The date was May 6, 1937, exactly a year after *Hindenburg* commenced regular transatlantic service. The death toll was 36 of the 97 persons on board. This tragedy effectively marked the end of rigid lighter-than-air vehicles (for purposes other than advertising automobile tires).

During the era of dirigibles, free balloon ascents were still fairly popular. The emphasis was on discovery, and balloonists turned to high altitude flights. The Swiss-born twins Auguste and Jean Piccard spearheaded this conquest of high altitudes. Their solution was to attack the upper atmosphere in sealed and pressurized gondolas instead of in the vulnerable open baskets used by early pioneers like Henry Coxwell.

The use of an enclosed gondola was a significant advance, because it eliminated much of the danger of high altitude ascents. Initially, aeronauts would take in oxygen through a hand-held tube, but this arrangement brought tragedy. Altitude sickness caused blackouts and death when the tube slipped from the mouth. Later, oxygen masks and pressure suits solved these problems, but the pressurized gondola allowed an aeronaut to ascend to greater altitudes without the encumbering equipment needed for open basket flights.

The Piccards made their first balloon flight in 1913 from Switzerland, across Germany to France. During their 16 hours aloft, the Piccards made a number of scientific measurements and developed a lifelong interest in balloons.

After World War I, the Piccards left Switzerland, Jean moving to America to continue his education and Auguste to Belgium to accept a physics professorship at Brussels University. Auguste began his gondola experiments in Belgium with the aid of a grant from the *Fonds National de Recherches Scientifiques*. Construction of the balloon and gondola began in Augsburg, Germany.

While Auguste Piccard was designing and building his gondola balloon, the last of the open basket altitude seekers was attempting to push the records even higher. He was Hawthorne Gray, a Captain in the US Army Air Corps. In 1927 he exceeded the existing German record by ascending above 42,000 feet. Unfortunately the record was not accepted, because Gray had been forced to parachute from his balloon basket and altitude record rules demanded that an aeronaut return to earth with his balloon.

In November of 1927 Gray tried again and did manage to

reach 42,470 feet. However, his oxygen breathing apparatus and scientific instruments iced up in the deep cold at that altitude and Gray perished from lack of oxygen. Tragically, his body returned to earth with his balloon and he was credited with the record.

Gray's death had two effects on Auguste Piccard—it cautioned him and convinced him that an enclosed gondola would be the only route to space flights by balloon. It was May of 1931 before Piccard was satisfied with his balloon's design and performance. He and Paul Kipfer ascended from Augsburg to an altitude of nearly 52,000 feet. Despite problems encountered with the gondola's machinery and instruments, Piccard and Kipfer landed safely on a glacier in the Austrian Alps.

What followed was a flurry of altitude records and record attempts. In August 1932 Auguste Piccard ascended with Max Cosyns to 53,139 feet, and in 1933 two Americans, T.G.W. Settle of the Navy and C. Fordney of the Marine Corps, pushed the record to 51,221.

In October of 1934 Jean Piccard and his wife Jeanette ascended to 57,579 feet, a women's altitude record that stands to this day. A year later Captain Albert Stevens and Captain Orville Anderson of the US Army ascended to 72,377 feet, a record that stood for 21 years. From that point, Air Force Captain Joseph Kittinger began parachuting from incredible altitudes, first from 76,000 feet and finally 102,800 feet in 1960.

In 1961 two Navy Commanders, Malcolm Ross and Victor Prather, reached 113,733 feet, the accepted record at the time of writing this book. The gondola came down in water and Prather was drowned during the recovery operation, an event that lead to the use of frogmen in recovering manned satellite vehicles a few years later.

In 1966 Nick Piantandia made an attempt to break Kittinger's parachute record. After reaching an unofficial altitude of 123,000 feet he discovered that his oxygen mask regulator was frozen and returned to earth without jumping. Unofficially, this is the highest altitude reached by a manned balloon.

This craving for altitude was pioneered by the Piccards. Their instruments gave science its initial data on radioactivity, atmospheric electricity, cosmic rays and other outer space-related phenomena. The pair developed the closed gondola and the use of multiple balloons. They also helped to develop plastic balloons that eventually lifted other aeronauts to altitudes exceeding 100,000 feet. Jeanette Piccard continued her interest in space flight and subsequently became a consultant to the National Aeronautic and Space Administration.

The scientific activities of the Piccards spanned several generations and the family still maintains its ballooning affiliations. Jean and Jeanette Piccard's son Don is now a manufacturer of hot air balloons.

It is significant that most of the high altitude flights had expenses underwritten by either the military or by public grants. Until the advent of hot air balloons a few years ago, ballooning was simply too expensive for more than a handful of very affluent individuals. The cost of hydrogen gas was great, while to fill a balloon bag with helium was even more expensive.

The public use of balloons dwindled at about the time that Count von Zeppelin perfected his rigid lighter-than-air craft. At the turn of the century, the Wright brothers were evolving and testing their heavier-than-air machines. The airplane was born and rapidly progressed to the point where balloons were left to the few affluent free spirits who had no desire to drive through the sky in a noisy, bumpy contraption made of wood and medal.

Within 20 years of their first successful flights, both fixed wing and rigid lighter-than-air craft had conquered the Atlantic. A free balloon had not made the journey, but the lure was still there. As you will recall, both Wise and Lowe had planned to fly the Atlantic and had even made abortive attempts.

So strong was the lure of the Atlantic that Edgar Allan Poe, then an unknown newspaper reporter, used it to pull off a great deception. The New York *Sun* bannered a headline on April 13, 1844—**"Astounding News! The Atlantic Crossed in Three Days! Signal Triumph of Mr. Monck Mason's Flying Machine!"**

Mason was actually a noted aeronaut of the time. He had accompanied Green in the *Nassau* on the first cross-country flight of 480 miles in 1836. A year before Poe's hoax, Mason had successfully flown a 44-foot model dirigible powered by a clockwork motor.

Poe, still some years from his success as a suspense writer and down on his luck, needed money badly. Having heard of Mason's successful model, he bilked the *Sun* out of a considerable sum for the "exclusive" story.

According to Poe's fanciful tale, Mason's balloon *Victoria* crossed the Atlantic in 75 hours, landing near Charleston, S.C. Eight men had supposedly made the flight, but Mason's machine had the same problem of all other early dirigibles— lack of an adequate powerplant. Such a flight as Poe imagined was impossible in 1844.

During the decades below and after the Civil War, Wise and Lowe made their unsuccessful attempts in free balloons. In 1873 P.T. Barnum apparently was able to inflame one of his circus' traveling balloonists into attempting the Atlantic. The man, Washington Donaldson, ascended from Brooklyn, New York, en route to Paris, making it as far as New Canaan, Connecticut, before aborting his flight. A few years later Donaldson and Wise drowned in Lake Michigan. They were on a training flight for another projected assault on the Atlantic at the time.

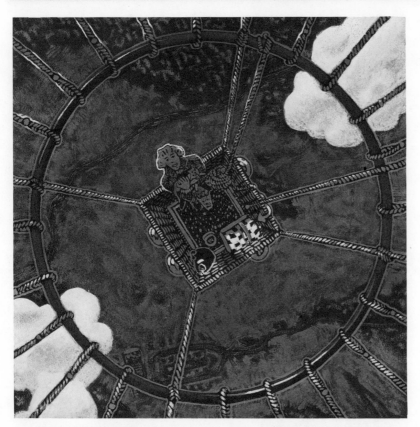

It was 1910 before another attempt was made in a lighter-than-air vehicle, this time in a dirigible. Walter Wallman, an American newsman, left Atlantic City with five fellow adventurers and a small kitten. Bad weather, the villain in most serious transatlantic attempts, was Wellman's downfall. Fortunately, the adventurers had a wireless radio on board. They were able to abandon their craft 375 miles out and hitch a ride back on a conveniently passing ship.

While wind layers in the North Atlantic blow predominently from west to east, the more southerly trade winds move in the opposite direction. Just before World War I a free balloon attempt was planned via these trade winds. The 500,000 cubic-foot *Suchard* encountered inflation and equipment problems, however, and was never launched.

The next serious attempt came later in 1958. Armed with modern equipment, a four-person team of Arnold and Tim Eilart and Colin and Rosemary Mudie was defeated by the weather and to some extent by a lack of oxygen breathing equipment.

The British team prepared *Small World* with appropriate emergency equipment, including a lifeboat-like gondola and chemicals for manufacturing fresh hydrogen gas from sea water.

Two times during the flight, gas needed to be vented from the balloon to prevent death at high altitude. Both times *Small World* was caught in violent updrafts accompanying thunder storms. Gas was generated after the first incident, but the second time too much gas was vented and the balloon crashed to the sea approximately halfway between the starting point in the Canary Islands and the West Indies, the flight's goal. The crew calmly set sail westward in their gondola/lifeboat and finished the journey!

Ten years later two movie stuntmen, Jerry Kastur and Mark Winters, made an attempt from Nova Scotia. They suffered the most frustrating of fates. Only 50 miles from their launch point, the pair was becalmed and had to be rescued by a passing boat.

An attempt in 1970 ended in death for three adventurers,

Malcolm Brighton and Rodney and Pamela Anderson. Their *Free Life* crashed to sea after 29 hours, and no trace was found.

With the advent of inexpensive private aircraft, the balloon had fallen into disuse. Air-minded individuals could fly their own fixed-wing aircraft much less expensively than a gas balloon. Except for occasional record attempts and scientific flights, balloons had virtually disappeared. Only a very few were being flown for pleasure.

BASICS OF BALLOON FLIGHT
2

The theory of balloon flight is directly related to the concept of using an envelope to trap gas which is lighter than the surrounding air. The principle dates back 2500 years to Archimedes.

As balloon pilots know, the atmosphere is heavier, or more dense, at sea level than it is at higher altitudes. An increase in altitude to 18,000 feet, for example, results in a corresponding decrease in atmospheric pressure of about 50 per cent. Essentially, there is a pressure continuum—called a *pressure gradient*—starting at sea level and dropping in density as altitude increases.

A hot air balloon acts as a "pressure gradient detector." There is more pressure at the lower part of the envelope than at the top, so the balloon tends to rise. It would seem the pressure differential between the top and the lower portion of the balloon would be insignificant. The difference, however, is substantial in a balloon 70 feet in height. The balloon envelope acts exactly like an air bubble rising to the surface from the bottom of a lakebed.

Both gas and hot air balloons are similar in operational theory. The gas version consists of a closed envelope containing a gas—usually helium or hydrogen—that is "lighter" than the atmosphere. In contrast, the hot air balloon envelope is open and it contains warmed air which is "lighter" than the ambient atmosphere. The bottom of the envelope is left open to permit the introduction of more warm air from the burner each time the balloon loses lift from air cooling in the envelope.

In contrast to hot air balloons, gas aerostats are relatively difficult to control in flight. Gas balloons can only descend by venting gas to lose lift, and they ascend by releasing sand or ballast to change the lift-to-load ratio. As a gas balloon rises, it will reach an equilibrium altitude and remain there until a change takes place in the lift-load ratio.

The most common change encountered is in temperature, either because of a colder ambient air or a loss of solar heat. When the balloon cools, the gas contracts and the aerostat begins to

. . . gas balloons are relatively difficult to control in flight.

descend. In order to control this descent, sand must be jettisoned until the balloon again reaches equilibrium. The limitation with this method is in the amount of gas and sand that can be carried on board. A gas balloon flight must be terminated when too much gas has been valved off, or when ballast is running low.

Hot air balloons, on the other hand, are more maneuverable, because relatively rapid changes in lift can be made without affecting the flight's duration. Hot air balloons carry a fuel—usually propane—which heats a burner to quickly provide additional lift. The balloon can quickly lose altitude merely by venting off some of the hot air from within the bag. Both of these procedures can be done much more quickly and economically than with a gas balloon.

Various conditions effect the available lift of a hot air balloon. As noted above, the primary lifting force in balloon flight results from a density differential between ambient gas and gas within the envelope. Thus, hot air balloons require less temperature to fly in cold air than in warm. Humidity also influences available lift. Fixed-wing aircraft can develop more lift in dry air than when it is humid, and this principle also applies to hot air balloons.

. . . hot air balloons require less temperature to fly in cold weather. . .

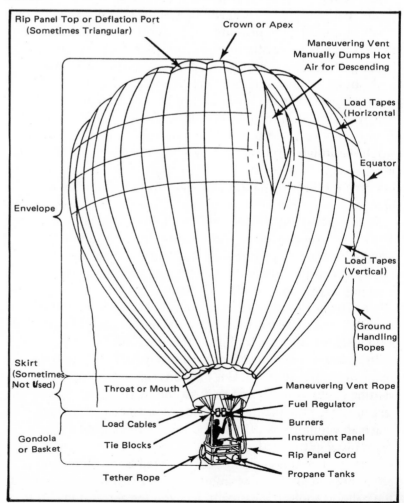

Lift is also lost with increasing altitude. As the atmosphere thins out, it becomes more difficult to maintain a density differential between the inside and outside air. This is particularly noticeable if an ascent is to be made to a high altitude, because burner efficiency decreases by approximately four per cent per 1000 feet over the Mean Sea Level (MSL). Cold fuel tanks also reduce fuel pressure and burner efficiency as ambient air temperature nears 40 degrees Fahrenheit.

The amount of lift developed is more than a simple theoretical consideration. In addition to the above factors, lift is effected by the weight of the balloon plus its passengers. Since fuel consumption is closely related to these considerations and flight conditions, a flight can be shortened by 25 or 30 per cent of its normal duration when these combined factors come into play.

One final factor influences the theory of balloon flight. Since an aerostat travels with an air mass, the horizontal direction and velocity of each flight will depend entirely on the wind. Vertical direction and velocity can be controlled, but horizontal travel is totally at the whim of the elements.

BALLOON FLIGHT BASICS

In ballooning, theory and practice are somewhat at variance. Since we are concerned here with hot air balloon flight, we will leave the practice of gas ballooning to others. This is not because of a dichotomy between the hot air and gas ballooning enthusiasts, however. In truth, most hot air balloonists are anxious to gain experience in gas balloons, and it is probably fair to say that to hot air balloonists, gas ballooning is the ultimate in aerostat flight.

The reasons hot air balloons have virtually replaced gas balloons in the United States are two-fold. First, hydrogen—although an excellent lifting gas—is extremely explosive (remember the *Hindenburg?)* and has been little used for manned balloon flights in this country. And second, helium—also a good lifting gas—is so expensive that one flight would cost several thousand dollars.

Hot air balloon flights usually take place shortly after sunrise or shortly before sunset because air movement is usually at a minimum during these hours. Mornings are usually preferred because the air is cooler and the balloon has more lift. As the day progresses and the earth is warmed by the sun, uneven heating of the land surface causes wind to rise. Coupled with thermals and other vertical currents, this results in very poor flying conditions. It is sometimes possible to fly in the late afternoon after the wind has died down, but such flights always carry with them the possible hazard of running out of daylight.

An open launch site is usually chosen—especially on the downwind side—so that nothing will be contacted by the balloon on take off. It is also wise to choose a place which is large, fairly flat and without sharp objects which might tear the balloon or impede the inflation.

helium . . . is so expensive that one flight could cost several thousand dollars.

Bill Reynolds

Once a suitable launch site has been found, the balloon is laid out and spread with (in some models) the maneuvering vent down, so air pumped into the balloon cannot escape through the vent. The basket is laid on its side, and crew members are stationed at the mouth of the balloon to hold it open. There are several methods for putting air into the balloon. The most popular is to use a motor-driven fan. An alternative is to have one to three crewmen take hold of the mouth of the balloon and inject air into it by flapping the top of the mouth up and down.

The balloon fuel and heat system should be fully checked prior to hooking up the envelope cables. This should include a "snif test" and a test firing of the burners. As soon as the balloon has been puffed with cold air, the burner is activated and the blast valve cracked open. The resulting flame is much like a blast furnace. While heat is being shot into the balloon, members of the ground crew are stationed around the bag to hold the mouth open so it will not get in the way of the flame. As the balloon fills with hot air, they will let it slowly rise.

If the flame contacts the fabric, it will immediately melt a hole. Seldom does this hole abort a flight, but such burn damage is expensive and troublesome to repair.

The propane fuel used in the burner is not as unpredictable as it might first appear. One should remember that it must escape from the tank, mix with air, and contact flame before it is volatile. In the event of a leak, usually only a local flame results. Rarely does it suddenly explode out of control. One possible fire danger does exist on very cold mornings, however. Tank pressure can become a problem and propane will not necessarily vaporize as it comes out of the pilot. Under such a circumstance, it will occasionally drip and ignite on the floor of the basket.

As the balloon comes to an upright position, the man on the blast valve moves back into the basket to keep the balloon from taking off. The other members of the crew hold the basket in place.

Two other methods of inflation are occasionally used. In one, short bursts of hot air are put directly into the envelope. In the other, a separate hand-held heater, called a "weed burner," is used in place of the regular burner.

Once the balloon is upright, the pilot goes about checking his equipment, hopefully from habit. He looks up into the bag to make sure the envelope is in proper position, ensures the vent and deflation lines fall down into the basket, checks the cables to see that none are twisted or otherwise out of place, examines the panels and basket, and tests the nuts and bolts to make sure all are in place and tight. He will look up to make sure that the vents are closed and the balloon is a sealed unit, and before take off he will re-check all the fuel connections.

The pilot then turns to his instruments, setting the altimeter to field elevation or to some other convenient setting from which he can later measure his distance above the ground. He turns the

Bill Reynolds

Once the envelope is unpacked (this page) and spread out (opposite page), the basket is tied down to the chase car. This helps keep down the number of run-away balloons.

Bill Reynolds

Once the envelope is inflated, wind can cause the balloon to tip. Note the effect of the wind on the envelope.

variometer to zero, and notes the temperature indicator to be certain the balloon heat is within safe operating limits. This indicator measures the temperature at the top, or apex, of the balloon. This area is subject to the most heat.

The aeronaut then scans the fuel gauges—normally located on top of each of the propane tanks—to make sure they are functioning properly and that he has adequate fuel for the planned flight. He observes the pressure gauge on the regulator, usually setting it to about 80 pounds per square inch. This insures the flow of fuel will be at a proper pressure and will mix sufficiently with the incoming air at the burner. FAA regulations also require that the balloon carry a compass, although this is of little value to a balloonist who has minimal control over his direction of travel.

Some balloonists carry radio equipment so they can communicate with their ground crews, but most do not. If the pilot plans radio communication, he will have a trial run with his radio gear before ascent.

Although the steps preceding a flight might seem to be cumbersome, in practice they can be handled rapidly and efficiently. In any event, let's assume the inflation procedure has gone well and the balloon is now ready for flight. The pilot cracks open the blast valve. This again sends flames shooting up into the center of the balloon. During flight, the blast valve is either entirely on or entirely off, and this results in either a good deal of noise or complete silence.

As the burner blasts and the balloon starts to gain lift, the pilot will constantly monitor the temperature. Based on his prior knowledge and experience, he will have a good idea how much heat is required to cause the balloon to lift off. He will consider air and envelope temperature, humidity, weight of balloon and passengers, take-off altitude and wind conditions.

When the temperature rises to that point where he would expect it to lift the balloon, the pilot will give the command "hands off." In ballooning language, this means to very carefully let go of the basket to determine buoyancy, but to stand ready to grab it again. This enables the pilot to determine how light his balloon is, and he may do this several times during his preparation for takeoff.

Under ideal conditions, the basic idea is to take off slowly. In order to clear high tension wires, buildings or other obstructions in the near vicinity, however, it may be necessary to get the balloon fairly hot and accelerate the ascent. But it is only through the experience gained from many takeoffs that a pilot learns how much lift is needed. Even under less than ideal conditions, beginning an ascent with excess lift should be avoided, because it puts severe horizontal stress on the envelope.

After the pilot takes off, it is usually his intention to ascend to an altitude and stabilize. He rises to a certain point and establishes equilibrium at that altitude. After stabilizing, he again uses the blast valve to heat up the balloon and start another ascent. This is called "stair-stepping," and it is the preferred method of both ascending and descending in perfect control. Short bursts on the blast valve are more effective than long bursts. Most balloon students are inclined to blast too long, and then wait too long between blasts. This results in a tendency toward over-reaction, both while ascending and descending.

When the blast valve is opened in a balloon, the response is markedly different from the response of a car or airplane when the throttle is advanced; there a throttle gives a fairly immediate response. When the blast valve is turned on, there is a delay of 15-30 seconds before the balloon shows any indication of responding to the additional heat. The heat is supplied 50-60 feet below the apex of the balloon, and it requires time to rise inside the envelope. This time lag between opening the blast valve and any visible response from the balloon depends on the size of the balloon, the output of the burner, and the combined factors of temperature, weight and humidity. Once a balloon starts to rise, it may continue to ascend for 1000 feet or more after the blast valve is shut off.

It is difficult to overemphasize the variances that will be experienced in balloon handling characteristics as a result of factors such as ambient temperature, envelope temperature, humidity, weight and altitude. These factors are constantly changing during the course of a flight, and each change results in a handling variance. When the balloon goes up, an increase in altitude tends to give it decreasing lifting capacity. As the day wears on, the surface air will become warmer and less dense. The weight of the balloon will constantly decrease as propane is used during the flight. These changing factors are compensated for by a certain "feel" the pilot develops as he gains experience.

One of the most important aspects of flying is not to let the balloon "get ahead of you." This happens when the pilot fails to concentrate on flying. A short attention lapse can cause the balloon to start descending faster than anticipated. When this happens, it can take a surprisingly long time to "turn the balloon around" and start ascending.

With inexperienced pilots, this happens a great deal, because they have not learned the proper blasting rhythm. Even with experienced individuals, this occasionally happens while they are changing from one propane tank to another, or taking photos. Keep in mind that as the balloon descends, cold air is rammed into the open mouth, causing the balloon to accelerate to terminal velocity. Most competent pilots spend a good deal of time flying level or at constant rates of ascent or descent.

It takes an experienced balloonist to bring his balloon down to a soft landing—lightly touching the earth, skipping across the surface if wafted by a light breeze. The ability to make a spot landing efficiently can be important to both life and equipment. When it is necessary to land in a limited area, it is better

... it is better to have a hard landing on the right spot than a soft landing in a lion's cage.

to have a rapid, bone-jarring landing on the correct spot than a soft landing in the lion cage at a zoo.

For descents, the maneuvering vent can be opened to expel hot air. It closes automatically, and only a few seconds with the maneuvering vent open will cause the balloon to start a reasonably rapid descent. As a rule, the maneuvering vent is not used a great deal, because escaping hot air must be replaced with bursts from the burner. (This is an uneconomical use of propane and shortens the length of the flight.) Pilots must be able to use the vent not only when descending, but also to check a too rapid ascent.

During a flight, the pilot has fairly effective control over the vertical direction of the balloon. He has very limited control, however, over the horizontal movement. What little horizontal control he does have is based on his ability to locate an air mass moving in a desired direction and to stay within it. Even experienced airplane pilots often fail to appreciate the differences in air or wind movements at various altitudes. It is not uncommon, for instance, to find wind moving west at an elevation of 300 feet and east at 600 feet.

When balloonists have a preferred direction in which they would like to travel, they usually make a high altitude ascent, noting on their way up the various points at which wind changes occur. They then descend to the desired altitude and ride the wind in the direction they choose. A wind shear (the boundary layer at which winds going different directions meet) is usually discernible as the balloon goes through it. With experience, a pilot learns the feeling of a momentary fresh breeze and a shuddering as the balloon passes through air layers moving in opposite directions. Jacques Charles, the pioneer gas balloonist, used a different method of determining wind shears aloft. He would merely release a small hydrogen-filled balloon before launching and carefully note its behavior as it rose out of sight.

Most balloonists prefer to fly at an altitude of less than 400 feet, because at low altitudes they can best observe activity below. Much low flying is done during pilot training, as this is the most important skill a balloonist can possess. It is a challenge to fly for several miles with the basket never higher than 5-10 feet.

If bushes, shrubs, or small trees are encountered, the balloon can usually fly through them with no damage to either, but power lines are extremely dangerous. Two rules are generally observed when approaching power lines—the balloon should be either 1) sufficiently high or ascending at a rate of at least 200 feet per minute, so if the burner fails the balloon is carried clear, or 2) sufficiently low that the deflation panel can be pulled and the flight terminated well before the power lines are reached.

As noted in Chapter 1, passengers are instructed during all landings to face in the direction of travel, to bend their knees slightly on impact with the ground, and not to leave the basket while landing. It would seem unnecessary to tell passengers not to fall out, but it *has* happened. If a passenger climbs or falls out, the balloon becomes suddenly lighter and will abruptly take off.

A high-wind landing is an adventure in itself.

A high-wind landing is an adventure in itself. A balloon lands at the same speed as the wind is blowing, so if the wind speed is 30 knots, the landing of the balloon will also be at 30 knots. Even landings with a five-knot wind tend to be rather exciting.

The preferred technique for making high-wind landings is to level off at an altitude of 10 to 30 feet and then pull the deflation line. This is a red rope or strap which hangs down into the basket. When it is pulled, a large panel of the balloon opens and it descends rapidly.

The deflation port is different with each balloon model. In some, it is a triangular panel that starts at the top and runs down near the equator. The deflation port is often held in place with Velcro, and when it is pulled, hot air escapes very rapidly.

As a balloon lands, the envelope tends to form a sail, so in high-wind landings the basket might be dragged along, making it difficult for passengers and crew to stay in. A balloon can drag the basket for hundreds of feet in a high-wind landing particularly if the deflation line is not fully pulled.

Safe ballooning is no accident. Although this young man looks like he's in a precarious position, he is strapped in securely with heavy-duty webbing. He is also wearing a helmet, another must for safety.

After flight, the bag is deflated (upper photo). But before the envelope is returned to its bag (below), the remaining air must be squeezed out of it (left).

A word should be injected here about the operational limits of the hot air balloon. The fabric from which the envelope is made should not be heated above the manufacturer's recommended level. If it *is* heated beyond that limit, it will not come apart on the spot, but the fabric will be permanently weakened. If the temperature at the apex approaches the red line, action should be quickly taken. This normally involves landing and letting one of the passengers out to lighten the load. If it is a very hot day, flying may even have to be discontinued. Due to the danger of fabric weakness, apex thermometers should be calibrated frequently.

Operational ceilings for balloons are limited in much the same manner as they are for other aircraft which do not carry oxygen. It is not normally advisable to maintain an altitude above 10,000 feet without oxygen. Some balloons do carry oxygen equipment for special high-altitude flights, but this is not common. It is dangerous to have oxygen near the burners and the extra weight of such equipment will necessitate additional lift.

Maximum ascent and descent rates are established by the manufacturer. Such rates assume that the envelope is in good repair and has not aged beyond its operational limits. Generally it is better to use a lower ascent and descent rate in order to provide a safety margin.

GETTING
ALOFT
3

In the previous chapter, we touched briefly on a typical balloon flight. Now we are ready to go into detail about each of the procedures necessary to make a successful and enjoyable ascent. Ballooning is not limited to seasonal or geographic considerations. Weather permitting, it is an all-season and all-terrain sport. With proper planning, ballooning can be done almost anywhere that it is not expressly prohibited by FAA regulations. Apart from the obvious times, places and conditions when ballooning would be dangerous, it is usually possible to find suitable take off and landing sites even in mountainous regions.

Experience has shown that there are several requirements for safe and successful balloon flights. At least one FAA-rated balloon pilot should be on board, along with several mature and experienced helpers. Extra equipment is also needed: area chart, tether rope, repair tape, safety line, igniters, tools and appropriate wrenches. The balloon should have the proper aircraft documents on board, including a Certificate of Airworthiness and a Registration Certificate. The pilot in command (PIC) is required to carry an appropriate pilot certificate as well. A suitable transporting vehicle, or a trailer with an approved hitch, brake system and electrical connections, is another must.

INSTRUMENTS AND ACCESSORIES

Federal Aviation Regulations (FAR 31.85) require that several basic pieces of equipment be carried on each hot air balloon. These include an altimeter, variometer, fuel quantity gauge, compass, and envelope temperature indicator. Additional desirable equipment (some of it required by flight manuals) would include protective head gear, sparkers, safety line, map, radio, transponder, gloves and fire extinguisher.

Altimeter. This is essential for compliance with the FAA altitude requirements of controlled and noncontrolled airspace. Unlike the airplane pilot, however, a balloonist customarily sets his altimeter for a ground level reading at take-off. Since balloon

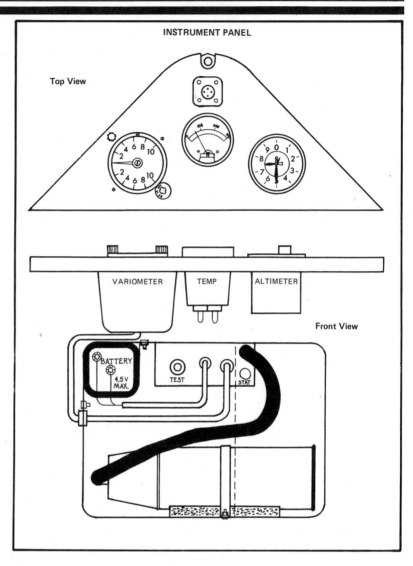

INSTRUMENT PANEL

Top View

VARIOMETER   TEMP   ALTIMETER

Front View

BATTERY
4.5 V
MAX.

TEST   STAT

Raven Industries

flight is customarily slow, any man-made or natural obstacles in the line of flight are easily avoided.

Variometer. A balloon can only be controlled vertically, and the variometer indicates velocity up and down. The standard rate-of-climb or electric variometer allows a pilot to maximize this control. Such instruments are almost essential at altitudes above 1000 feet, because from that point it is difficult to "feel" descent or ascent due to a lack of visual reference points.

Envelope Temperature Indicator. This is often called a *pyrometer.* The fabrics of all certified balloons are "red-lined" at a set maximum temperature. The temperature indicator consists of a sensor in the crown of the balloon, which is attached to a gauge in the basket.

Compass. This instrument is not of great significance for a short hop on the pilot's home turf, but on extended flights over unfamiliar terrain, it is sometimes helpful. In this case, it should be used in conjunction with map reading and/or radio guidance from the chase vehicle.

Fuel Quantity Gauge. Each tank has a gauge which indicates the percentage of fuel remaining. Experienced pilots make frequent reference to this instrument.

Protective Headgear. Most flight manuals designate this item as "required" equipment, but its value does not become obvious until one experiences a jarring, high-speed landing.

Sparker (or matches or lighter). Occasionally, the pilot light of the burners will extinguish in flight, and sparkers (igniters) become essential.

Safety Line. A safety line at least 150 feet long allows the pilot to throw out a rope to helpers on the ground to slow down a fast landing approach. It also permits a person on the ground to "walk" a becalmed balloon out of an otherwise inaccessible landing place.

Radio or Transponder. Simple citizen band radios can be of great assistance in directing the chase car to a landing site. Conventional aircraft radios are uncommon in balloons, but are of obvious value around airport traffic areas. Transponders are generally used only in conjunction with planned flights to altitudes above 18,000 feet.

Gloves. Heavy leather gloves are necessary due to the possibility of hand contact with the burners.

Fire Extinguishers. Whenever there is a large supply of fuel and a nearby open flame, there is always a danger of losing control of the combustion process.

TO FLY OR NOT TO FLY

Because of the capricious and unpredictable nature of weather, it is essential to obtain up-to-date weather information from the nearest Flight Service Station (FSS), or by monitoring the Transcribed Weather Enroute Broadcasts (TWEB) shown in the Airman's Information Manual. Particularly important are surface

> . . . its value does not become obvious until one experiences a jarring landing.

winds, winds aloft and the local area forecast, but *all* weather factors should be taken into consideration.

A direct reading on winds in your launch area may be obtained by releasing a small, helium-filled balloon just prior to making the decision to fly or not. If the indicator balloon ascends straight up and does not move laterally, the flight should be delayed or postponed. (The balloon would probably be becalmed after take off.)

If the indicator balloon begins to move horizontally away from the launch site at a speed of greater than eight miles per hour, cancellation of the flight should be seriously considered. The same action would be in order if the indicator follows an erratic course which would be consistent with severe gusts, thermals, or up and down drafts in the air above the launch site.

Before landing

Loose equipment. . . . . stowed
Gloves/helmets . . . . .secure
Surface wind . . . . .observe
Fuel tanks. . . . . .secure
Ground crew . . . . .visible
Passenger impact briefing and landing instructions . . . complete
Road proximity. . . . . accessible
Angle of descent . . . . reasonable
Obstructions . . . . .clear
Safety line. . . . . .out
Fuel tank valve . . . . .loose
Deflation port line. . . . . .clear
Burner at ground contact . . . . off

At landing

Maneuvering vent (no wind) . . . . .open
Deflation port (no wind). . . . . .open
Fuel tank valve . . . . off
Fabric . . . . protect from burner

After landing

Fuel pressure. . . . . bleed
Envelope . . . . hold mouth closed/squeeze to apex
Instruments. . . . . .off and/or stowed
Envelope. . . . . .pack in bag
Basket. . . . . pack/load in vehicle
Landing site. . . . . .checked and clear
Trailer. . . . . .secure

At the time weather information is obtained, the FSS should be informed of your flight plan as nearly as you are able to predict it. It also helps the FSS to know the size, color and markings of your aerostat. Flight Service, if requested, will pass this information on to other FAA jurisdictions, including Approach Control.

After the balloon is upright, there are a few other checks that can be made, such as checking the maneuvering vent for operation, visually checking the deflation cable for kinks and tangles, and making sure the instrument calibrations are done.

The apex crew member may be positioned out a little away from the balloon, or far out at the end of the apex rope. His duty is to correct any rolling of the balloon from side to side by pulling the apex rope in a direction opposite to the roll. During cold inflation, he should straighten the load tapes where they join at the apex.

He should also keep the balloon lined up straight with the basket. Once the balloon is being heated and begins to upright itself, he can control the speed with which it rises by applying restraint according to the PIC's instructions. If the balloon rises too quickly, it will rock back and forth.

It is best to have the crew rotate positions at each inflation so they learn to work every area of the balloon. If there are enough crew members available, the extra members should stand behind the basket during inflation to view the inside of the balloon and the working of the burners. Later, this will be helpful to them in understanding how to correct problems and more effectively work their stations.

After the balloon is upright the crew should keep the skirt away from the burners by holding it out with either the skirt ropes (not the vent rope) or by the hoop inside the skirt. The crew should be standing by to keep weight on the basket until lift off time. Crew members should visually check the entire system, including gore-by-gore inspection for tears and damage. Damage can be noted by gore number.

Once the balloon is upright, stable and in no danger of drag, a final check of items used in flight can be made, final instructions to crew given, and final instrument calibrations made. The pilot opens the maneuvering vent to check its workability, visually follows the deflation cable to the top of the balloon while checking for tangles or kinks, observes the top of the balloon for openings and examines maneuvering vent lines for tangles or knots. If passengers are to be taken, they are briefed on landing position and procedures, staying in the basket, helping in flight by checking surrounding obstacles, fuel readings, ground crew progress and other in-flight details.

Even with several years of ballooning experience, it is possible to neglect one or two points in the inflation procedure. Here is a handy checklist that should help eliminate the problem:

Designate a crew chief if one is to be used. Also designate persons to be responsible for driving chase vehicles, picking up inflation gear, operating the radio or using hand signals. Make sure keys are in the car and that chase vehicles have sufficient fuel and propane.

A rendezvous point or emergency telephone relay number should be designated in the event of a lost balloon or separation of the crew. The PIC should also give the crew an idea of his flight plan. As an example, "Will fly for one hour and land. Will be doing touch and go's, and picking up passengers."

FLIGHT CHECKLIST

The PIC is responsible for the condition of the aerostat, the safety of passengers and crew, and the conditions of flight. He also must observe all applicable Federal, state and local regulations governing balloon flight. To ensure that these matters are not overlooked, the following checklist should be used prior to every flight. The item on the left requires the response or action on the right.

Pre-flight assembly

Fabric . . . . intact
Deflation port . . . . sealed
Maneuvering vent . . . . sealed
Tangent lines . . . . clear
Connecting pins/rings . . . . secured
Fuel tanks . . . . full
Fuel lines . . . . secured
Pressure test . . . . sufficient
Leak test . . . . sniff and listen
Blast valve . . . . free
Instruments . . . . operating
Maps and helmets . . . . on board
Sparker and wrenches . . . . on board
Safety line . . . . on board
Envelope bag . . . . on board
Basket . . . . intact

Instruct the crew as to your particular preferences and method of inflation. And during cold inflation, take the time to walk around the balloon and check each crew station, explaining to each individual once more what he is to do. This is much appreciated by the crew.

All crew members working around the balloon should wear gloves. This prevents rope burns and punctures to fabric. Members working around the mouth should also wear helmets.

Instruct the crew members never to walk or stand on the fabric. If it becomes necessary to walk on the envelope, shoes should be removed. The balloon should only be worked on the load or gore tapes—never on the fabric—and then only with the amount of pull stated by the PIC.

Ropes should never be wrapped around hands, arms or legs. People have been carried aloft in this manner. Also tell the crew to keep clear of the load tapes, ropes and basket.

The layout area should be checked for sharp objects that could tear or puncture the fabric, and no smoking can be allowed around the basket or the fabric. If a ground-wind indicator or flag is to be used, a crew member should be designated and instructed in its use.

Radio or ground-to-air signals should be coordinated before lift off, and signals should be thoroughly explained. An emer-

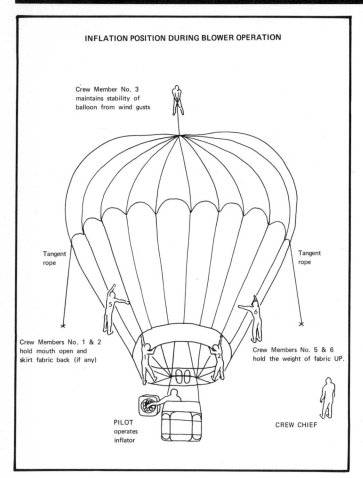

INFLATION POSITION DURING BLOWER OPERATION

Crew Member No. 3
maintains stability of
balloon from wind gusts

Tangent
rope

Tangent
rope

Crew Members No. 1 & 2
hold mouth open and
skirt fabric back (if any)

Crew Members No. 5 & 6
hold the weight of fabric UP.

PILOT
operates
inflator

CREW CHIEF

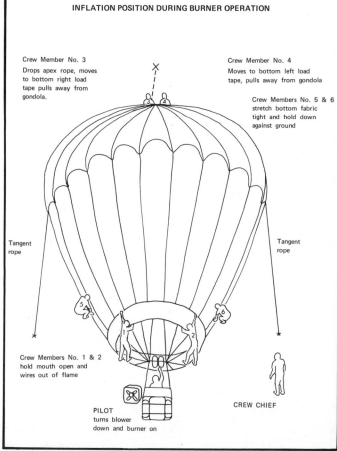

INFLATION POSITION DURING BURNER OPERATION

Crew Member No. 3
Drops apex rope, moves
to bottom right load
tape pulls away from
gondola.

Crew Member No. 4
Moves to bottom left load
tape, pulls away from gondola

Crew Members No. 5 & 6
stretch bottom fabric
tight and hold down
against ground

Tangent
rope

Tangent
rope

Crew Members No. 1 & 2
hold mouth open and
wires out of flame

PILOT
turns blower
down and burner on

CREW CHIEF

gency cut-off signal should be determined and the crew instructed when to use it.

A crew member should be placed in charge of collecting loaned gloves and picking up tools and equipment used during the inflation. If the balloon carries a supply of gloves and tools they should be marked with the name or color of the balloon to which they belong, especially if several balloons are launched together.

A crew member should be assigned the responsibility of loading the inflator, checking the tie-downs on the chase vehicle and cleaning up the field after inflation.

Other considerations for a safe flight include adequate crowd control at both launching and landing sites. Spectators should be kept far enough away from the balloon that a sudden landing after lift off —or a quick change of course when landing—will offer no danger to them.

Prior to launch, permission of the owner to use the launch site should be secured. The launch site itself should consist of a flat surface of at least 100 feet square, free of stubble and debris, with sufficient clearance of buildings, trees and power poles. Areas of ground covered by dry grass are hazardous and should be avoided. At launch, the wind velocity should not exceed eight miles per hour.

PREFLIGHT PLANNING

Safety in flying is no accident—it exists only with careful and thorough planning. Good anticipation either prevents accidents or enables the pilot to effectively handle unexpected conditions and emergency situations as they arise.

Because the human memory is fallible, a written preflight check list is helpful. A comprehensive checklist is shown in this chapter but there are several items the pilot in charge (PIC) should cover prior to each flight.

He should brief all crew members of their duties, potential hazards, and the importance of their jobs. An envelope layout should be made with the deflation port (if any) at the bottom, and the bottom side stretched tight. The pyrometer (if appropriate to the balloon model) should be installed. The maneuvering vent and the deflation panel must be sealed, and the steel cables must be untangled and the connecting clamps separated.

Next, make certain the skirt (if any) and hoop are correctly installed. The deflation "red line" must be free, as should the maneuvering vent line. An inspection report on fabric conditions should be made by all crew members, and envelope clamps should be connected to the gondola. Finally, a burner should be positioned as close as possible to the envelope mouth, and at least one full tank of propane should be on board.

BRIEFING THE GROUND CREW

Ballooning is a group sport, and the crew is an essential, integral part of it. Nothing is more essential for an enjoyable and successful flight than a well-trained and well-instructed ground crew.

Nothing is more essential. . . than a well-trained and well-instructed crew.

Before a flight, they should be briefed because crew and pilot cannot hope to work effectively together unless each knows what the other will be doing.

Since balloonists are individualists, each pilot tends to have his particular preferences for flight procedures, and the crew should be thoroughly briefed before every inflation. Although this procedure often takes a half hour to complete, an efficient launch team will be able to inflate in less than 10 minutes.

Safety in all phases of balloon operations is a paramount concern, so crew members, spectators and the owners of launch and landing sites are entitled to optimum protection against all damage. Balloon and equipment layout, rigging and systems checks should be made by the PIC, or by an assistant under the PIC's direction. All final checks are the responsibility of the PIC.

When briefing the crew, the PIC should take into consideration that most individuals do not absorb and remember everything that is said to them. The pilot should repeat the instructions and ask the crew to repeat them until the message is clearly understood. This will insure a better inflation and a more confident crew.

Some pilots prefer to designate a crew chief (CC). The CC is usually an experienced crew member, a student pilot, or another pilot. The PIC should clearly express to the CC what his responsibilities will be, since these may vary according to the number of crew available and the weather conditions. A PIC may choose to have an experienced CC brief the rest of the crew while he is checking systems.

No crew member shall take the authority of the PIC or contradict his instructions. The responsibility for safety and success is that of the PIC alone, but a well-trained crew can be helpful in reporting problems and interacting with each other to carry out the launch responsibilities.

INFLATION PROCEDURE

Drawings in this chapter clearly indicate the position of each ground crew member during the inflation procedure. Crew members assigned to the mouth keep the envelope, skirt and cables out of the flame and heat area. As the balloon rises, crew members hold everything away from the flame and check all cables and ropes for twists or kinks. The two short ropes at the top cable division can be pulled out and the skirt can rest on top of them during the uprighting process. During a windy inflation, the PIC may prefer to attach the red deflation line to the belt loop of the crew member on the side of the envelope mouth. Or, if the deflation line is to be attached to the basket, instruct that crew member to be ready to pull it on signal.

While the balloon is being laid out, the crew member assigned to the fan should check the gas cylinders for leaks. Usually this is done by sniffing for escaping propane while the valves are all

. . . an efficient launch team will be able to inflate in less than 10 minutes.

tightly closed. He should then turn the burner away from the balloon and start it for testing purposes, or for warmup during the cold months.

Inflation begins by flapping the laid-out envelope full of air by means of quick, up and down scooping movements with the bag mouth, or more commonly, by blowing air into the mouth with a motor-driven fan. Once the bag has been filled with cold air, the burner is turned on and hot air is injected into the balloon.

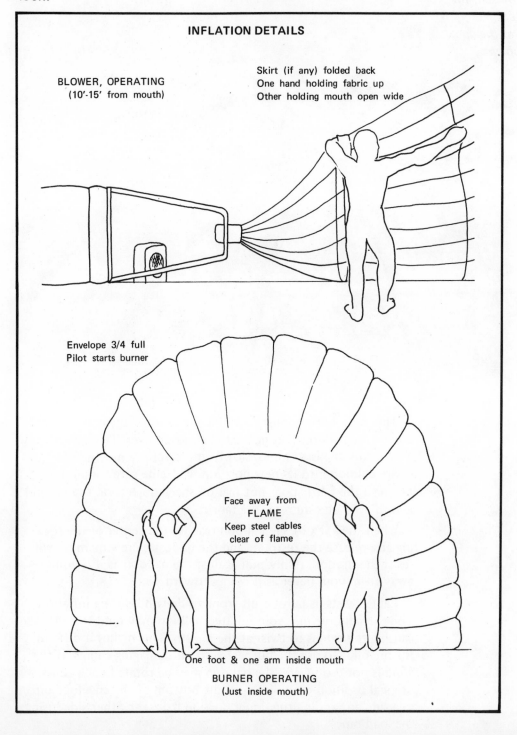

INFLATION DETAILS

BLOWER, OPERATING
(10'-15' from mouth)

Skirt (if any) folded back
One hand holding fabric up
Other holding mouth open wide

Envelope 3/4 full
Pilot starts burner

Face away from
FLAME
Keep steel cables
clear of flame

One foot & one arm inside mouth

BURNER OPERATING
(Just inside mouth)

CORRECTING INFLATION PROBLEMS

Should the wind come up or change direction during inflation, it can cause one side of the balloon to cave in—or push the fabric inward—making it difficult to fill the envelope with cold air. More crew members on that side to pull the fabric out is one solution, but if the wind is too strong it could be necessary to shift the entire basket and envelope so that it is lined up directly downwind.

If the top of the balloon opens at any time during inflation, the pilot should be notified. Many balloons have Velcro at the apex, so re-sealing is no problem.

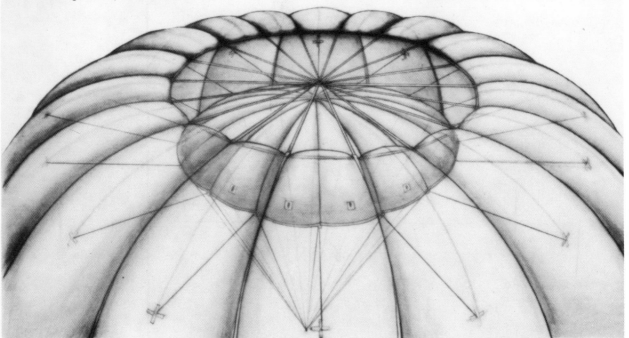

This is best accomplished by having most of the crew on the side of the balloon that needs to be moved over. The crew firmly grasps only the load tapes, slowly and carefully moving the entire balloon into its new position. Extreme care should be taken so the fabric does not tear on sharp objects on the ground and that no one steps on the fabric.

When the apex of the balloon reaches the center of the rocking arc, release the restraint and the opposite crew member will resist the motion. (Only pull against the balloon as it is going away from you, never as it comes toward you.)

Cable twists usually result from a side wind during inflation. The partially or fully cold-inflated balloon may tend to roll, causing the cables to twist at the mouth. This makes it difficult for the pilot to use the burners without damaging cables. If the wind is not too severe, the balloon may be rotated back to its original position by pulling out the bottom of the envelope on one side and rolling the upper portion from the other side, using the load tapes.

The apex crew member can also help stabilize the rolling by use of the apex rope. If the wind is too severe to roll the balloon back to its original position, it may be necessary to roll the basket over in the direction that the balloon has already turned. This requires several persons at the basket to keep it properly positioned.

If the top opens at any time during inflation, the pilot should be notified. In this case, it will be necessary to pull the balloon down and re-seal the Velcro. If the top opens while the balloon is fully upright, the envelope must be cooled until it can be pulled down. To correct this problem, simply re-seal the Velcro and resume the inflation procedure.

When the balloon is upright, rocking can occur from ground wind or from the balloon coming up too rapidly. Usually it will settle by itself, but if the pilot wishes it stabilized, this can be done by the use of tangent and apex ropes. Crew members position themselves on all ropes or on the ropes at opposite sides of the balloon and in line with the rocking motion. As the bal-

The dark lines that divide the envelope below into sections are called load tapes. These should be inspected before going aloft.

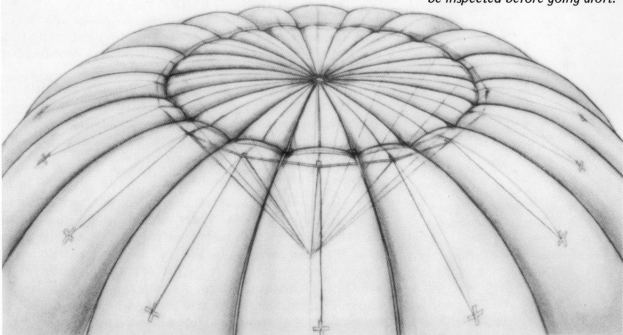

loon rocks away, restrain by pulling against it and feeding the rope out slowly.

EMERGENCIES

The most important thing for a crew member to know in case of emergencies is the cut-off signal to the pilot. This is usually a hand-across-the-throat movement. Depending on the type of in-flation (windy, in a small area, etc.), the pilot should always brief his crew on this and other emergency procedures and about any problems he may anticipate.

The red deflation line should always be located where it is easily accessible. An inflation should never begin when it is still inside the balloon or out of reach. Crew members should visually inspect inflation sites and be aware of any potentially dangerous obstacles and make note of how much clearance is available to a partially or fully inflated balloon.

Should a balloon start to drag before it is upright, everyone should know how much drag room is available. Once a partially-inflated balloon begins to drag, inflation should immediately cease. If the pilot wants to continue the inflation (the success of which is doubtful), it should be continued only if the area is safe. Depending on the circumstances, the pilot may wish to attach ropes to the basket and an anchor point, or have the crew run with the basket until the envelope is full, buoyant and hot enough to eliminate "false" lift.

If for any reason the pilot should be away from the basket and a drag or other dangerous situation develops, the person nearest the red deflation line should use his own judgment as to whether to wait for the pilot's return or deflate the balloon immediately. It is always better to be safe than sorry, and most pilots would prefer to abort an inflation rather than risk damage or an accident. The top can always be resealed and inflation begun again. And if the inflation is that difficult or tricky, it is probably better to wait for another day.

An envelope with its ropes and cables conducts electricity. If the balloon should be in contact with power lines, no one should touch any portion of it. Crew members should keep bystanders away. Should a balloon be draped over power lines and touching a fence, the fence should also be avoided.

ADDING WEIGHT TO THE BASKET

In winter and on cooler days the balloon will reach equilibrium and flying temperature at a lower envelope temperature than usual. The fewer the occupants (and the lighter the weight), the lower the flying temperature will be. The pilot may wish to have the crew add more weight to the basket until he is ready for lift off. Other situations can occur in which he will want weight added. These include launches in high ground wind, in small launch fields, or in confined areas where the pilot will want to clear obstacles by climbing rapidly on take off.

The pilot may ask several crew members to hold the basket down by adding some of their weight. Or, as the balloon heats, he may ask one crew member to try to lift the basket to indicate its relative weight. When buoyancy is achieved, the pilot may request to have the balloon held down. This is done by having one or two crew members restrain the basket with their arm strength only.

When the pilot asks for weigh off he wants all hands removed.

Crew members adding weight or assisting around the basket just prior to lift off should take care not to become entangled in any ropes, or to allow themselves to be in a position where they cannot get away from the basket at lift off.

PRE-LAUNCH

It is often assumed that "propane is propane." But this is not particularly true in winter when water may condense in the fuel system and cause malfunctions by freezing. During cold weather, propane has a greatly diminished vapor pressure, and fuel pressure determines burner output. Hence, a balloon with a 350-pound payload may be quite responsive to the addition of heat when the ambient temperature is 70 degrees, but extremely sluggish when the temperature is 10.

Some balloonists suggest warming the tanks indoors prior to winter flights. This is an acceptable practice only if the tanks are sufficiently insulated to allow little heat loss during the flight. If this is not the case, the pilot might take off with a very responsive fuel system and find after two or three hours of flight that the responsiveness is too slow to permit safe ballooning. A number of balloonists keep their tanks in insulated covers.

It is the pilot's responsibility to make sure his crew is protected. In this photo, for example, the ground crew is wearing gloves and the flight crew is wearing helmets.

Envelope fabric and Velcro need to be checked regularly for integrity and strength. There are precise methods for checking both of these. If they tear or come unfastened under minimal hand pressure, the fabric and Velcro are weak.

The top should be checked immediately prior to inflation. Even though it was secured at the end of the previous flight, it is essential that the preflight procedure include another careful inspection.

All persons on board are in close contact with vital portions of the balloon. For this reason, each passenger should be treated as if he was a crew member. Instruction should be given concerning the operation of the balloon, the importance of not handling the red deflation port line, not loosening the fuel tank straps, and not pulling the maneuvering vent line unless instructed to do so by the pilot.

Prior to takeoff, crew members should be shown the procedure for bracing themselves at the time of landing. They should be shown how to keep their knees bent and to grip the sides of the basket which will not come in contact with the ground when the balloon touches down. Sides which may contact the ground if the basket tips over should also be avoided.

If there is a brisk wind at the time of landing, passengers should be advised to brace one foot against the downwind side of the basket. This will help prevent being thrown against the side of the basket if it topples over on impact.

The crew should wear appropriate clothing and protective gear, including gloves, long-sleeve shirts and helmets with visors or goggles. All of these are important, but eye protection is particularly vital when the flight is over a wooded area. The possibility of eye injury from the branch of a tree coming in contact with the basket is ever present, especially when landing.

The balloon commander is, of course, responsible for all aspects of the flight. He must be completely familiar with the aerostat and any special considerations or conditions that might pose a hazard to safety. He should also be certain the crew members are in emotional harmony with the prospect of flying in a balloon. It could be disasterous to allow a passenger on board who is obviously frightened or apprehensive. It is also unwise to fly with a passenger who is unable to follow directions.

LAUNCH

All tethers should be prepared so they are firmly attached until the pilot gives the release signal. No external weight should be allowed to remain on the balloon during the time the pilot is testing for the temperature required to establish equilibrium. After this is determined, the pilot may request one or more crew members to add their weight to the outside of the basket. This keeps the balloon from taking off as heat is added. At the release signal, the balloon will rise from the launch site at a brisk rate.

Taking off with excess lift is particularly important if obstacles are close to the launch site, or if wind shears are present. Such shears can force hot air out of the balloon shortly after takeoff, causing it to dip suddenly. The practice of allowing a ground crew to attempt to "shove" the balloon up into the air is unsafe, for it can lead to a sudden landing at an inopportune site just after lift off.

IN FLIGHT

Even though every attempt should be made to obtain the best weather information prior to takeoff, weather conditions during flight may take a sudden and unpredictable change. If fog, smog, powerful wind gusts, thermals, wind shears, or precipitation and lightning are encountered, it is wise to land as soon as possible.

Another weather consideration is becoming becalmed over potentially hazardous landing sites. If air currents at high and low altitudes cannot be found, the pilot might descend to a level where it is possible to pull the balloon toward a more desirable landing spot with the ground handling line. If becalmed over water, it may be possible to have a power boat tow the balloon to the nearest shore with the ground line. There the aerostat can be deflated without allowing it to be completely immersed.

Balloons equipped with a maneuvering vent may be able to gain minimal horizontal motion by opening the vent. This limited push can occasionally help to position the balloon over a favorable landing site.

POWER FAILURE

Power failure is an ever-present possibility. It can result from being unable to relight after a flame out, having to shut down the burner because of a fuel system leak, or running out of fuel. The chances of any of these mishaps occuring can be reduced by maintaining the fuel system in top condition and not attempting to stretch a flight beyond the limits of the fuel on board.

When power failure does occur, the principal danger is not from the rapid rate of descent (usually not more than a parachute's speed), but from landing in a place where damage to the balloon, passengers, or to persons and property on the ground is likely. If the combined drift and descent course indicates a collision is imminent, it is possible to increase the rate of descent so as to land short of the obstacle. To do this, the maneuvering vent line should be pulled or—if close to the ground—the deflation port should be opened.

THE CHASE CREW

The chase driver is an important member of the ground crew. He is usually the first one to arrive at the landing site, and his timing and assistance are of vital importance. The pilot should designate his chase driver prior to the planned flight. The chase driver should use the following check lists to instruct his chase crew:

The chase driver . . . is usually the first one to arrive at the landing site.

● **Before arriving at the launch site.** A full tank of gas for each chase vehicle and an extra propane tank for the balloon are the chase driver's responsibility. So are: protecting clothing, such as coveralls, gloves and boots; coffee or juice and food if the location is isolated. He should have with him large-scale road maps (section, county and Forest Service) as well as a tow rope and a small shovel.

● **Upon arrival at the launch site.** The chase driver should brief the crew on its duties during inflation. Next he requests the intentions and expected duration of flight from the pilot. Finally, he asks for a volunteer navigator to accompany the chase crew.

● **During the chase.** He should obey all safe driving rules, and be courteous to other drivers. Fast driving is seldom necessary. He stays on a road parallel with the balloon's flight path, and doesn't try to outguess the pilot. If he decides to land and expects assistance, the pilot will drop his safety rope and/or signal his intentions. Otherwise, the driver assumes the flight will be continued. He also pays particular attention to the time the balloon has been airborne for an indication of fuel quantity.

● **Post-Flight.** Directing recovery to minimize crop or property damage, the chase chief should caution spectators to stay back until all equipment is in a safe location. He should also caution the crew and bystanders about trespassing. Over-enthusiastic spectators are apt to forget property owner's rights.

The crew members should be reminded the fabric is fragile and will tear and puncture easily, and everyone must take care not to step on or walk on the balloon fabric. The deflation line, vent rope and instrument panel thermometer connections should all be disconnected from the basket.

Fuel should be turned off, lines bled and burners cooled. The remaining air should be squeezed out of the bag and the top re-sealed. The envelope can be lap-folded or rolled and stuffed into the bag.

Packup should be accomplished as quickly as possible and a check of the field should be made for tools, equipment and any litter. People and vehicles should spend no more time in the landing area than necessary, and only the recovery vehicle should enter the landing site.

Only after all the work is done should the balloon toast begin. The celebration of a safe flight would not be complete without the traditional champagne which is supplied by the aeronaut and shared with spectators and crew alike.

Diplomacy. Remember that we fly only as long as the local populace enjoys our presence. Our welcome can be easily abused and refused.

Greet everyone with a smile. Don't hesitate to ask onlookers to participate in activities, but be sure to assign them easily understood tasks. No one should be allowed to remain a stranger.

Remember that we fly only so long as the local populace enjoys our presence.

Answer questions and help everyone who is interested in our fascinating sport.

Pay particular attention to members of the communication media. They can do much to promote ballooning. Above all, remember that the farmer's land is his livelihood.

PRE-LANDING

Just prior to landing, several items should be covered. Despite preflight instructions, passengers should be reminded to face the direction in which the balloon is moving. They should also be cautioned on the severity of the landing shock. For safety, loose objects in the basket—wrenches, igniters, gloves, cameras—should be secured.

Wind velocity should be noted and an appropriate landing site chosen. This should be of sufficient size, and with a minimum of obstructions. It is especially vital to avoid landing sites with power lines downwind, or with exposure to high-speed freeway traffic. Choose a field near an access road, but with no hazard to people, crops, livestock or buildings.

As the balloon descends, the ground crew can be directed to the best landing site access roads by voices or hand signals. The safety rope should be dropped only if the chase crew is on hand. The blast valve *must* be turned off before ground contact, and one hand kept on the deflation line.

LANDING TECHNIQUE

At one time or another, a balloonist will be faced with the necessity of landing in turbulent air. When this happens, the landing should be attempted in the middle of the largest available field. This will allow the greatest leeway to cope with wind forces which could cause you to miss the landing site by hundreds of feet. Choosing a landing area is best done at very low altitudes, but to attempt to cruise at 100 feet in the presence of thermals is difficult. Dropping small pieces of wadded tissue paper from the balloon will provide valuable information about the wind direction and the air below. If the paper is wadded into a small ball and tossed out, it will fall rapidly and furnish the correct information.

Normal landings are the result of good judgment of altitude and smooth technique in using the blast valve to level off before touch down.

Run-on landings are required when the wind speed is 5-8 m.p.h. Gondolas can be skidded on the ground if weight is shifted to the side opposite the landing direction. To reduce bouncing and skidding, the maneuvering vent may be held open from just before ground contact until movement stops.

High-wind landings require a longer landing distance and a low angle of approach. The balloon should be leveled off at 10-20 feet and the red deflation line pulled all the way out before ground contact.

The chase crew should be aware of the necessity of asking and obtaining permission of landowners at the landing site. It is also important for the chase crew not to assist a balloon which has come down and is still in contact with power lines. If such a situation exists, chase crews must be certain that spectators are kept away from the balloon.

DEFLATION

During calm weather, deflation should not be attempted until the ground crew is available. The only exceptions to this rule occur when: fuel is exhausted, the wind causes parachuting, or a hazard exists from proximity to power lines or buildings.

Low-wind deflation requires ground handlers to know the direction of the envelope fall. They must be in a position to pull the apex downward and away from the burners. The burners should be sufficiently cool to preclude the possibility of envelope damage from contact with the fabric. Actual deflation consists of opening the deflation panel to its fullest, turning the basket on its side, and holding the envelope mouth closed. Tank valves should be closed and excess gas can be bled with the blast valve.

DISMANTLING AND STOWAGE

Balloon landings invariably attract spectators who are always happy to help with the balloon. Their help can very easily be used in dismantling and stowing the balloon.

If tied to the gondola, deflation and maneuvering lines are released and stowed. The envelope is then separated from the gondola and the cables are kept from tangling. Instruments are removed and stored in a safe place.

The envelope is gathered toward the center in 3-4 foot-wide strips, and excess air is rolled out from the mouth to the apex.

The envelope is then gathered from the apex to mouth in a wide pile, and put in a storage bag. The storage bag is covered, laced tightly and placed upside down in the basket. Next, all the components are secured in the transporting vehicle and firmly tied down.

The landing site and deflation area are policed for mislaid equipment. Double check the deflation site, because more than one ballooning day has been ruined by forgetting equipment and personal items.

EMERGENCY PROCEDURES

High impact landings usually result either from fuel exhaustion at high altitudes or plain poor judgment. If fuel is available, the blast valve is left on until just before touch down, but it must be off at touch down. Quick decisions must be made to pull the red deflation line, which should be snapped to your belt in case impact throws you out of the basket. Remember that if the burner is left on and you are not in the basket,

Balloon landings invariably attract spectators who are always happy to help . . .

the balloon will take off without you. And you are liable for all damages resulting from fire or collision.

Power Line contact can usually be avoided or injuries minimized if the deflation port is at least partially opened in flight, regardless of altitude. The rate of descent will be affected by the altitude and the degree of opening, and a quick vertical descent may avoid serious consequences. Contact with two wires generates enough heat to burn large holes in the envelope. Steel cables supporting the basket are easily burned on contact with high tension wires, and could result in occupants being spilled to the ground. Falling out of the basket and contacting any two wires (or one hot wire and a ground) will quickly result in multiple burns.

When in doubt, pull the deflation panel and worry about balloon damage later. You should not jump out of the basket.

Water landings with any wind present require that the deflation panel be pulled if the basket is to swamp enough to act as a sea anchor. In the water, the pilot should get out with the red line in hand. It is important to learn in a controlled and supervised training program how a balloon reacts when it is landed in water. Should it be necessary to make an emergency landing in water, this experience will provide confidence. After landing it may be possible, as previously mentioned, to be towed to shore, or the balloon may be allowed to drift to the downwind shore. If high winds or seas are present, however, it may be necessary to abandon the balloon. Fuel tanks can be converted to flotation equipment by allowing the propane to be exhausted and then closing the valves. Even when full, the tanks will provide sufficient buoyancy to keep the basket afloat.

NIGHT FLYING

Most balloons are not equipped for night flights. Even if so equipped, flying in the dark presents particular problems of identifying potential landing hazards. And the chances of being becalmed at night are many. In short, night flying is strictly for owls.

If darkness is closing in and a suitable landing spot is not immediately available, the remaining daylight should be used to make as safe a landing as possible. This should be done even if it means landing in an area normally considered unsuitable. Power lines become invisible at dusk.

THE FUEL AND BURNER SYSTEMS
4

A typical two-man hot air balloon flying under average atmospheric conditions uses about 50 pounds (or 12.5 gallons) of propane per hour. This is equivalent to about one million BTU, or the amount of warmth put out by 10 home furnaces going full blast. Obviously, a lightweight and efficient heater system is necessary to supply this heat.

Various heat sources have been used over the years in hot air balloons. The earliest used straw and wood as fuel, and some more recent balloons have used kerosene. Almost all aerostats in use in the US today, however, use airborne heaters fueled with propane known as Liquefied Petroleum Gas (LPG).

At normal atmospheric pressure and temperature, propane is a colorless gas. Its vapor can only be detected by the peculiar odor which is added to all commercial propane, and which varies in smell from one refiner to another. At atmospheric pressure, propane boils at minus 42 degrees Fahrenheit. When confined in a closed container at normal atmospheric temperatures, however, liquid propane will vaporize until the pressure within the container reaches a certain level. That temperature-dependent level is between 50 pounds per square inch (at 30 degrees) and 150 pounds per square inch (at 90 degrees).

Propane costs from 35-80 cents per gallon (depending on where and in what quantity it is bought), and it's available in most towns throughout the country. In either its liquid or gaseous state, propane lends itself to the storage, transmission and control requirements of hot air balloons.

Because propane is so widely used, a great selection of reliable storage tanks, fuel lines, fittings and control valves are available. Except in the coldest weather, propane creates pressure which can be used to feed it to the burners, thus making a fuel pump unnecessary. And since propane burns very cleanly, it does not leave significant deposits on the inside of the balloon envelope, nor does it create substances which cause damage to the envelope.

FUEL STORAGE

Hot air balloons carry their fuel supply at ambient (atmospheric) temperature in tanks designed to withstand the resulting pressure. It is possible to build a fuel system which carries propane is non-pressurized containers at or below the boiling temperature of propane (minus 42º F).

Such a system could employ extremely light fuel containers, and would be useful for very high altitude flight, where weight is critical and the probability of the fuel containers being exposed to physical abuse is slight. Landing with fuel in such containers would be hazardous, however, and some sort of fuel pumping arrangement would probably be required to move the propane to the burner unit.

Most fuel tanks in use today are of a type designed for use either on lift-trucks or recreational vehicles. Most are manufactured by Worthington or Lennox, and the size most commonly used holds 10 gallons of propane when properly filled. These pressurized tanks, because they are designed to safely withstand up to 350 pounds of normal service pressure, are also strong enough to withstand the physical abuse to which they might be subjected during flight in a balloon.

The most commonly-used tank is hydrostatically tested to 1750 psi. It weighs 26.5 pounds and carries about 43 pounds (more than 10 gallons) of propane. It's made of aluminum, and is about three feet tall and a foot in diameter.

Another tank is a horizontal, stainless steel container about 14 inches in diameter and three feet long. It weighs 38 pounds and carries approximately 20 gallons of propane. Its principal disadvantage is that it costs about $360, compared to $180 for an equivalent aluminum tank. These stainless steel tanks are hydrostatically tested to 400 psi.

Propane tanks in balloons have two to four valves, and each performs a different function. Every tank has a main valve and a pressure release valve. The main valve is the one through which the propane flows to the burner. A dip tube runs from the bottom of this valve inside the tank and to the bottom, so that liquid propane flows through the valve.

If large quantities of vapor are withdrawn rapidly from a propane cylinder, the cooling effect of the vaporization cools the propane and lowers the vapor pressure and rate of vaporization. In this event, the pressure in the tank quickly drops to the point where the flow of propane to the burners is inadequate for flight. This is the reason liquid instead of vapor is withdrawn from the tanks. The propane is vaporized at the burner, where adequate heat is available.

Each propane tank also has a pressure-release valve to prevent the tank from bursting if the pressure exceeds a safe amount. The pressure release valve is usually designed and positioned so that it releases vapor, not liquid.

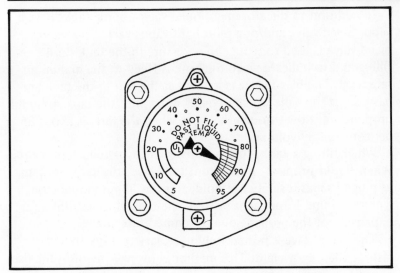

The red line on the fuel quantity gauge at left runs from 20-5 per cent. After the five per cent mark, the gauge is unreliable.

Pressure release valves on propane tanks are built to open when the tank pressure exceeds 375 psi. When enough vapor has been released to allow the tank pressure to drop below 375, the valve automatically closes. The pressure release on the stainless steel tanks mentioned above operates at about 273 psi.

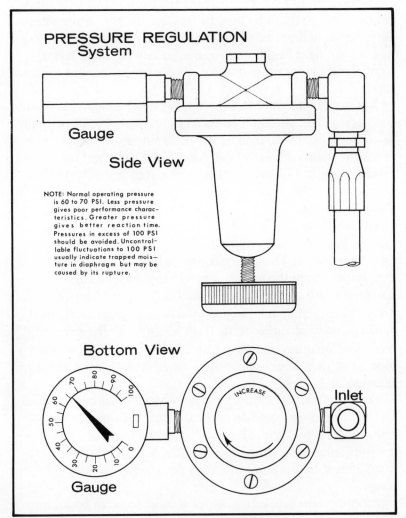

PRESSURE REGULATION
System

Gauge

Side View

NOTE: Normal operating pressure is 60 to 70 PSI. Less pressure gives poor performance characteristics. Greater pressure gives better reaction time. Pressures in excess of 100 PSI should be avoided. Uncontrollable fluctuations to 100 PSI usually indicate trapped moisture in diaphragm but may be caused by its rupture.

Bottom View

INCREASE

Inlet

Gauge

In addition to the aforementioned valves, some tanks have a vapor bleed valve and/or a pilot light vapor valve. The vapor bleed valve is used to reduce the pressure in the tank during refilling and to indicate when the tank is filled to the maximum safe level. The bleed valve is located at the top of the tank and has a short dip tube which extends down into the tank so liquid propane will flow through the valve when the tank is about 85 per cent full by volume.

When filling a tank, this valve is opened to relieve pressure. When liquid propane spurts from the valve, the tank contains as much fuel as it safely can hold, and the filling should stop. The remaining 15 per cent or so of the tank volume allows for expansion of the propane due to temperature change.

The bleed valve is not entirely necessary, because tanks can also be filled by weight. This method, however, requires the use of scales, which is often inconvenient. And if vapor cannot be released from the tank during filling, the pump used must be extraordinarily powerful to overcome the increasing pressure in the tank during filling.

Some balloons have a pilot light vapor valve which feeds vapor from the tank to a pilot light at the burner unit. Usually this is a needle valve so it can be used to regulate the size of the pilot light flame, and yet be completely closed when necessary. The vapor pilot light uses little propane, so tank pressure is not significantly reduced by drawing off propane vapor for the pilot light.

Various combinations of the valves described above are available as standard single units. As an example, the optional stainless steel tanks mentioned earlier use a single unit which combines the main tank valve, the vapor bleed valve and the pressure-release valve in a single valve body. The standard lift-truck or recreational vehicle tanks generally use separate valves to perform these functions.

All tanks used on sport hot air balloons have tank fuel quantity gauges, which are required by Part 31 of the Federal Aviation Regulations. These almost always indicate the quantity of fuel remaining in the tank as a percentage of tank volume. The gauges on vertical tanks usually read only from 35 down to five per cent, while the gauge on the horizontal stainless steel tanks mentioned earlier reads from 95 down to five per cent. Most fuel quantity gauges are unreliable. Therefore, a wise balloon pilot uses a backup method, such as timing the tanks, to measure fuel usage.

Propane fuel tanks must be securely restrained in the basket so they cannot jar loose on hard landings, injuring occupants or damaging the fuel lines attached to them. They must also be carefully protected from impacts with the ground or other obstructions if they are not of a type designed to withstand heavy abuse.

An important precaution which should be taken by all who

handle propane tanks is to avoid storing them inside closed buildings or carrying them in closed vehicles. If a propane tank is overfilled on a cold day, and then brought into a house or carried in a car, it might well valve off a large quantity of propane when the gas warms and expands. It can easily catch fire, with potentially disasterous consequences.

A defective or incorrectly calibrated pressure release valve could cause the same problem. This precaution is often ignored by many who handle propane tanks.

Tank filling is a slightly complicated process, but one which should be understood by all balloon pilots. Actual filling procedures vary depending on the valving arrangement of the particular tank being filled. Procedures for filling propane tanks are outlined at the end of this chapter.

FUEL TRANSMISSION

As easily ignored but important part of the fuel system are the fuel lines and their interconnecting fittings. The propane flows from the tank to the control valves and from the control valves to the burner unit through a combination of flexible hoses, metal lines and metal fittings.

Flexible rubber hose designed for use with propane is utilized wherever the fuel line must flex to avoid breaking. Usually rubber hose reinforced with steel mesh is used. The steel mesh minimizes the possibility that the hose will rupture from extreme abrasion or unusual tension being applied to it. Usually the flexible line is used throughout the system, except in the immediate vicinity of the burner, where heat might damage the rubber.

Metal tubing, usually stainless steel, is used close to the burner because non-metallic materials would not be able to withstand exposure to extreme temperatures. Because metal tubing will break if sharply bent, it is usually carefully supported and protected from anything which might bend it (such as stray support cables or the ground on landing).

Connection fittings on the lines throughout the system are usually brass or stainless steel, commercially available LPG, or high-pressure hydraulic line fittings. Such fuel line fittings require two precautions.

First, any series of fittings connected together into a long assembly with one end rigidly connected to a tank, burner unit or other relatively immovable part of the balloon are a significant hazard. If force is accidently applied to the free end of such a conglomeration, the fitting closest to the rigid attachment point is likely to break, due to the leverage of the combined fittings. Serious accidents have resulted from a failure to recognize and prevent this hazard.

A second problem arises with the "quick-release" fittings which are sometimes used in hot air balloon fuel systems to facilitate connection and disconnection of fuel lines. These have a history of unreliability. A quick-release fitting interconnects in such a way that moving a collar by a simple hand motion causes the fitting to disconnect. Most of these fittings were designed for use on compressed air lines. They were not designed to carry liquid or vapor propane, or to operate reliably at the extremely low temperatures that can result from propane vaporizing in the line at the fitting.

Further, such fittings can easily be disconnected unintentionally if brushed by the pilot or a passenger during flight or on landing. If one of these fittings fails to seal when it disconnects, a flow of propane—possibly of great proportions—is likely. Most balloon builders avoid using quick-release fittings on their balloons.

The LPG standards for propane tanks and fittings are quite high. Tanks and fittings must be able to withstand hydrostatic testing to 1750 psi. The standard maximum working pressure is 350 psi (fuel systems on sport hot air balloons are rarely, if ever, subjected to pressure greater than 250 psi). Of course, these standards apply only to commercially-available LPG fittings. Not all balloon builders use these.

FUEL FLOW CONTROL

Control of hot air balloons in flight is accomplished by the pilot varying the heat input to the envelope. As noted earlier, a two-man balloon flying under ambient temperature, humidity and loading conditions loses about one million BTU per hour. Because a balloon loses heat so rapidly, a descent will start quite soon if new heat is not added. An ascent, of course, is initiated by adding more heat than necessary to offset the cooling.

The heat output of a balloon burner is controlled by varying the rate of propane flow from the fuel tanks to the burner. During flight this flow rate can be varied from zero to some design-dependent maximum. In common practice, the maximum rate of fuel flow is usually small enough so propane flowing through the burner orifice has been completely vaporized, although this is not really necessary.

The basic means of pilot control of fuel flow, and thus heat output, is usually a lever-action blast valve. This valve operates either fully open or fully closed, and the balloon is piloted with a continuous series of open and closed blasts.

A needle valve is sometimes added to the burner system to allow the pilot to adjust the system to produce a constant heat output less than the maximum. This is known as a meter valve. All Raven balloons have this feature. Barnes, Piccard, Adams and Semco balloons have a blast valve which can be left partially open to give the same effect.

The meter valve is most useful for flying over farms and ranches where animals may be startled at the sudden roar caused by opening the blast valve. The meter valve is rarely used at other times, however, because of the constant roar of the burners when it is open.

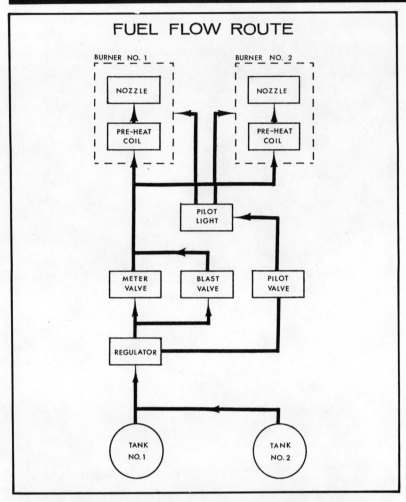

FUEL FLOW ROUTE

BURNER NO. 1

NOZZLE

PRE-HEAT COIL

BURNER NO. 2

NOZZLE

PRE-HEAT COIL

PILOT LIGHT

METER VALVE

BLAST VALVE

PILOT VALVE

REGULATOR

TANK NO. 1

TANK NO. 2

It is important to remember that any burner operating at less than its full output deteriorates rapidly.

Some balloons use a pressure regulator in the fuel system. This assures that the fuel flow—and thus heat output with the blast valve open—will be constant, regardless of variations in tank pressure due to changes in ambient temperatures from flight to flight. This tends to make piloting a bit easier, because the heat output from a given blast will be the same regardless of tank pressure (unless tank pressure is insufficient to supply the desired pressure at the regulator).

The disadvantage to regulators is that they contain a fabric-reinforced rubber diaphram which can unexpectedly rupture and leak considerable propane in flight. This has happened often enough (frequently with resulting onboard fires) to cause all but one balloon manufacturer to abandon the use of regulators. In operation, regulators should not be frequently adjusted, as this wears them out and defeats their purpose. A regulator which needs frequent adjustment is probably defective.

One manufacturer uses needle-valve trim controls on each burner, so that each can be individually adjusted.

Although the main tank valve's principle purpose is to allow the tanks to be removed from the system for storage and filling,

. . . any burner operating at less than its full output deteriorates rapidly.

Because of the heat given off by the burner, the cables that support the envelope must be made of heat-resistant steel.

it can, if necessary, be used as the principal control valve in flight. If a propane leak develops anywhere in the fuel system during flight, the pilot can close the main tank valves, set open all the other control valves in the fuel system, and pilot the balloon to a more or less normal landing by opening and closing the main tank valve to control the heat output of the burners.

In addition to these main burner controls, most balloons have a pilot light regulator or a needle valve to regulate the size of the pilot light flame. Some balloons have pilot lights which operate on fuel from the liquid fuel system, while others use a separate vapor line from one of the fuel tanks. The vapor system requires more plumbing, but it gives a quieter and steadier flame.

BURNERS

Hot air balloon burners perform three functions: vaporize the liquid propane supplied to them; mix the propane vapor with air to form a combustible mixture and burn the resulting mixture to form an essentially directional flow of very hot gases.

All burners commonly in use on hot air balloons have preheating coils surrounding the base of the flame. The liquid propane flows through these coils on its way through the burner. Since the coils are heated directly by the flame, they are not hot enough to vaporize the liquid propane flowing through them.

If the propane is not vaporized, it does not mix well with the air, and burns in a long, yellow flame which radiates a great amount of heat. Properly-vaporized propane burns with a mostly blue flame.

The vaporized propane flows out through a carefully-designed orifice which directs it toward and through the cylindrical coils where the preheating has taken place. The orifice usually divides the flow of vapor into individual streams, which then turbulently mix with the ambient air surrounding the orifice. The propane-air mixture is ignited by the pilot light and burns to produce a very hot flow of gases (a mixture of air and by-products of combustion which include water vapor, carbon dioxide, and small amounts of other gases.)

Some burners used on balloons built in the US have a cylindrical metal can—open at both ends—just within the preheat coils. This tends to direct the flame and to support and protect the preheat coils. It probably also tends to reduce the transfer of heat from the flame to the preheat coils, thus limiting the heating output of the burner unit.

An advantage of propane burner systems on balloons is that the fuel pressure can vary greatly without significantly affecting the efficiency of the burner. Of course, low fuel pressure reduces the flow rate and thus the heat output of the burner, but the heat output per pound of propane burned does not vary greatly.

Propane burners used in the US vary in maximum heat output from about four million BTU per hour to well over 22 mil-

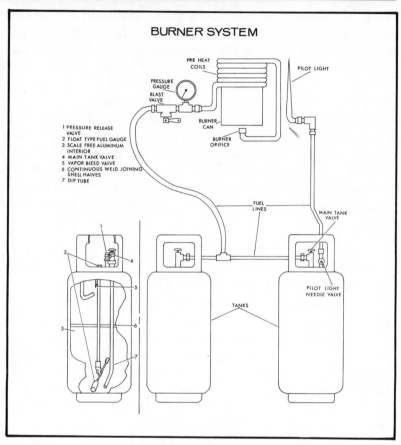

BURNER SYSTEM

1 PRESSURE RELEASE
   VALVE
2 FLOAT TYPE FUEL GAUGE
3 SCALE FREE ALUMINUM
   INTERIOR
4 MAIN TANK VALVE
5 VAPOR BLEED VALVE
6 CONTINUOUS WELD JOINING
   SHELL HALVES
7 DIP TUBE

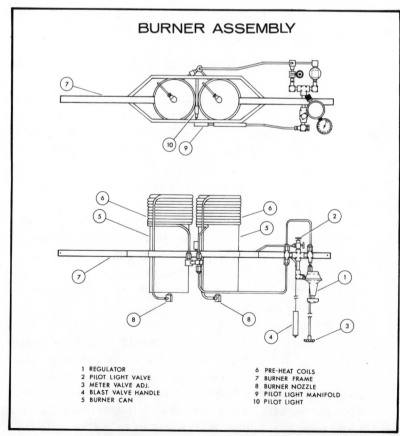

BURNER ASSEMBLY

1 REGULATOR
2 PILOT LIGHT VALVE
3 METER VALVE ADJ.
4 BLAST VALVE HANDLE
5 BURNER CAN

6 PRE-HEAT COILS
7 BURNER FRAME
8 BURNER NOZZLE
9 PILOT LIGHT MANIFOLD
10 PILOT LIGHT

lion. The more powerful burners result in somewhat safer balloons, since the greater rate of heat output available makes the balloon much more responsive and maneuverable. The current trend is toward burners which have maximum heat output in the range of 8-10 million BTU per hour.

FUEL MANAGEMENT

Good fuel management has two goals: to assure adequate heat is always available to properly and safely pilot the balloon, and to maintain an ability to cope with accidental fuel leaks. The techniques to accomplish these ends are by no means fully developed or widely agreed on by balloon pilots. There are, however, several basic rules which can help balloonists to cope with these problems.

The first is to always fly with one main tank valve open. The principal reason for this is that in the event of a sudden major leak in the fuel system, the pilot need only close one valve to halt the flow of propane. Also, if the pilot is forgetful and flies until he is out of fuel, he will still have a reserve in another tank with which he can safely land the balloon. And using tanks separately prevents an equilization of pressure.

With Bleed Valve and Pump

● Connect the hose from the fuel source to the main tank valve and turn on the pump.

● Open the fuel source valve (usually located on the fuel hose near the tank being filled), the main tank valve, and the vapor bleed valve. (The sequence in which these valves are opened is not important.) The tank is now filling.

● As soon as liquid propane starts to spurt from the bleed valve, close the fuel source valve, the main tank valve and the vapor bleed valve. Then turn off the pump.

● Disconnect the fueling line by slowly loosening the connection at the tank. The liquid propane in the line between the main tank valve and the fueling line valve will spurt out and vaporize (with the hazard of freeze burns). When this propane has finished vaporizing, complete disconnecting the fuel line.

Without a Bleed Valve and With a Pump

● Connect the hose from the fuel source to the main tank valve and place the tank on a scale.

● Turn on the pump and open the fuel source valve and the main tank valve. The sequence of opening these valves is again not important. The tank is now filling.

● As soon as the tank reaches its full weight, close the fuel source valve and the main tank valve. The full weight for any Certified by the Department of Transportation tank can be calculated from information displayed on the tank. All DOT-certified tanks have "water capacity" and "tank capacity" displayed on the tank. Water capacity is the weight of water the tank holds if

. . . if the pilot is forgetful and flies until he is out of fuel, he will still have a reserve . . .

it is filled to the brim. This is displayed on the tank immediately after the letters "WC." Tank weight is calculated with the tank completely empty and is shown immediately after the letters "TW."

To calculate the full weight, multiply the water capacity by the specific gravity of propane, which is approximately 0.5 (that is to say propane at 70 degrees F is half as heavy per unit volume as water). Multiply the result by 0.85, since propane tanks should be filled no more than about 85 per cent of their volume. This gives the amount (in pounds) of propane the tank can safely hold. Add this result to the tank weight to find the full weight for the tank. As an example, the most commonly-used vertical propane cylinder carries the following information: "WC 103.6 TW 26.5." The full weight of the tank is: Full Weight equals (103.6 x 0.5 x 0.85) plus 26.5, or 70.5 pounds.

● Turn off the pump, and carefully disconnect the fueling line as described in the final step of the procedure for filling the tank with both a bleed valve and pump.

The burner does three things: vaporizes the propane, mixes the gas with air and directs the burning mixture toward the envelope mouth.

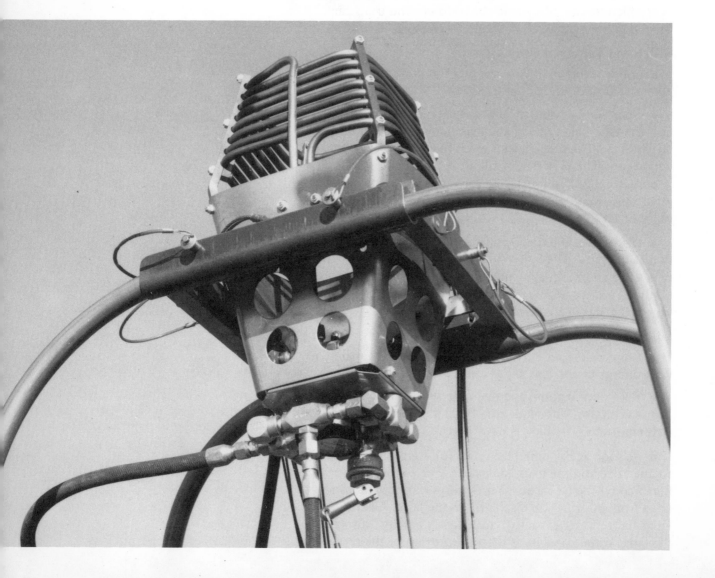

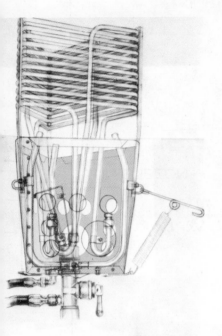

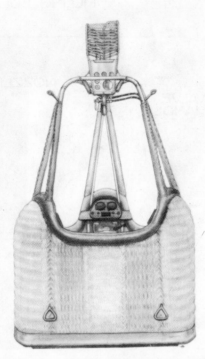

With Bleed Valve and No pump

This procedure is similar to the one with a pump. The method is very slow, but it is a way to transfer propane from one balloon fuel tank to another if necessary. It works best if the receiving tank has a pilot light vapor valve which can be opened in addition to the vapor bleed valve to further reduce the tank's internal pressure. The procedure is sometimes mistakenly referred to as "gravity feed."

Bleeding off vapor can easily reduce tank pressure by 10 psi, while tank height difference gives only 0.25 psi pressure difference per foot of height difference. As an example, 40 feet of height difference yields only 10 psi pressure difference, which is hardly practical.

Two further precautions should be observed during fueling. First, whenever propane lines are disconnected, they should be capped to prevent foreign matter from entering them. Common house flies are attracted by the odor of propane residue and will crawl into uncapped fuel lines. Inexpensive plastic caps are available for this purpose. Second, whenever propane lines are reconnected, they should be tightened and checked for gas tightness. Hand-tight fittings might not be discovered until an in-flight propane leak occurs.

Second, fuel should be managed so you will always land with several gallons in each tank. If a pilot exhausts the propane in all but one tank and then discovers that the remaining tank is for some reason unusable, he is suddenly and unexpectedly out of fuel.

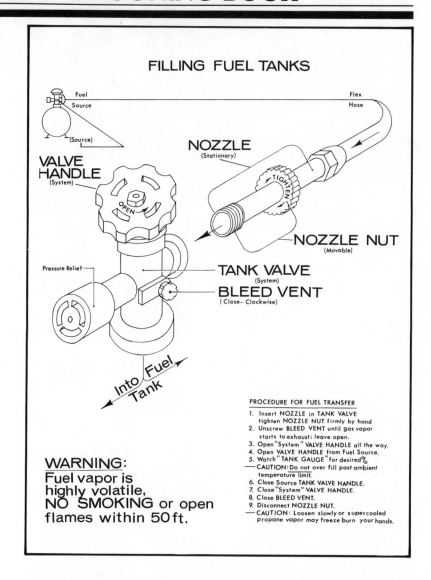

FILLING FUEL TANKS

Fuel Source

Flex Hose

(Source)

NOZZLE
(Stationary)

VALVE
HANDLE
(System)

OPEN

TIGHTEN

NOZZLE NUT
(Movable)

Pressure Relief

TANK VALVE
(System)

BLEED VENT
(Close- Clockwise)

Into Fuel Tank

PROCEDURE FOR FUEL TRANSFER

1. Insert NOZZLE in TANK VALVE
    tighten NOZZLE NUT firmly by hand
2. Unscrew BLEED VENT until gas vapor
    starts to exhaust; leave open.
3. Open "System" VALVE HANDLE all the way.
4. Open VALVE HANDLE from Fuel Source.
5. Watch "TANK GAUGE" for desired %.
—CAUTION: Do not over fill past ambient
    temperature limit.
6. Close Source TANK VALVE HANDLE.
7. Close "System" VALVE HANDLE.
8. Close BLEED VENT.
9. Disconnect NOZZLE NUT.
—CAUTION: Loosen slowly or supercooled
    propane vapor may freeze burn your hands.

WARNING:
Fuel vapor is
highly volatile,
NO SMOKING or open
flames within 50 ft.

A good habit to cultivate when preparing to switch from one tank to another during a flight is to add a good bit of heat to the envelope. The distraction from piloting to performing a tank switch is sometimes enough to allow descent to begin without the pilot's notice. If he is flying near the ground, power lines or trees, this distraction could result in a collision. Under some circumstances, the extra heat will not be necessary, but in any case it is better for the pilot to make an occasional exception to the rule when it is clearly warranted than to ignore the rule altogether.

Another good habit is for the pilot to time each propane tank as a check on the fuel gauges. Propane cylinder fuel gauges are not always reliable, so it is important for the pilot to have some other way to know how much fuel remains in a tank. If the pilot notes how long he has been flying on a particular tank, he will be able to figure out approximately how much time he has left on that tank, since the rate of fuel consumption can be roughly estimated even by a relatively inexperienced pilot.

Another good habit is to time each tank as a check on fuel gauges.

Jack Stewart

FUEL PROBLEMS

The two most common fuel problems encountered by balloonists are cold or contaminated propane. Cold propane tends not to supply the necessary vapor pressure to force the fuel from the tanks to the burners at a rate great enough to provide adequate heat output. The vapor pressure of propane is only 50 psi at 30 degrees, which is inadequate to safely fly some hot air balloons.

As mentioned earlier, some pilots warm their tanks indoors in cold weather so the vapor pressure will be sufficient, but this practice invites disaster. There is no ideal solution to the problem outside of flying with burners designed to operate at the lower pressures generated by cold propane. Of course, if the weather gets cold enough, no balloon can fly without being artificially warmed.

Gauges on tanks mounted in the horizontal position read from 95-5 per cent, while tanks mounted in the vertical position usually have gauges that read from 35-5 per cent.

In the US, LPG supplies are remarkably uncontaminated. From time to time, however, small amounts of water find their way into a balloon's propane tanks or fuel system. If the propane vaporizes at a valve, it is possible that it will freeze and form ice within the valve. When this happens, the effectiveness of the valve stem seal is destroyed and propane begins to leak at the seal.

Once a leak of this type and origin has started, it will rarely cease until the propane supply has been turned off or the valve is warmed to thaw the ice. Formation of ice by this means can also interfere with the functioning of pressure regulators. If a pilot believes there is water in his fuel tanks, he can prevent further problems by adding a small amount of methanol to the tanks. Methanol, which can be obtained from a propane dealer, acts as antifreeze and has an insignificant effect on the performance of the burners or fuel system.

FILLING PROPANE TANKS

Two basic precautions should be taken during all propane transfer operations: there should be no potential ignition sources within 50 feet of the spot where the filling is being done (no running motor vehicles and no smoking), and the persons doing the transferring should wear gloves to prevent freeze burns from vaporizing propane. Freeze burns have the same symptoms as heat burns; they can be serious and painful.

BALLOON MAINTENANCE
5

In the third century BC the principle that makes ballooning possible was discovered by the Greek mathematician Archimedes. He concluded that when a gas less
dense than air is enclosed in a container, the difference
between the density of the gas and the air it displaces causes the
container to rise. The modern hot air balloon operates on the
same principle, although it uses heated air instead of the lighter
gas. It does this for a very simple reason—economics.

To fill a three-passenger balloon with helium could cost about
$3000, while hydrogen would cost about $800. The bill for propane to heat a comparable hot air balloon would come to about
$20. Propane—with its vastly increased safety—is largely respon-
sible for sport ballooning's return to popularity.

Starting at ground level, the first component of each balloon
is the gondola or basket. Aeronauts are such traditionalists that
some trim their aluminum gondolas with wicker for the sake of
appearance. Wicker is a remarkably durable substance for its
light weight, but it is subject to embrittling and/or rotting with
age, and it can be damaged by being dragged over rough terrain.
Baskets should be checked regularly for signs of damage or loss
of resilience, particularly along the floor and at the attachment
points for the envelope cables. Aluminum or fiberglass gondolas
require less upkeep, but the welds should be inspected (especially
along the bottom) after hard use.

The propane fuel tanks for the burner are usually stored upright in the corners of the gondola or basket. The tanks can be
dislodged by hard landings, so they need to be looked at regularly to make certain they are secure and no leakage has developed
at any of the fittings. The fuel quantity gauge should also be
frequently checked to see that it is still operative. This gauge is
particularly important to the pilot, and occasionally it can be
stepped on or jarred out of commission.

The gondola will also contain a drag rope for landing, a tether
rope for restraining the balloon during launch, protective headgear to guard against jarring landings, heavy leather or asbestos

gloves for working around hot burners, a sparker for relighting the burners if they should flame out in flight (plus matches or a lighter as a backup for the striker), a portable radio and some current sectional charts. The latter are useful, not merely for navigation, but for identifying radio frequencies along the way. And for flights over 10,000 feet, portable oxygen should be available.

The absence of storage space in most baskets makes it essential that equipment be stowed carefully in place after each flight and checked again before departure.

An abbreviated instrument panel is usually located in one upper corner of the basket. The only required instruments for hot air balloons are a compass, altimeter, rate of climb/descent indicator (variometer), fuel quantity gauge and envelope temperature indicator (pyrometer).

The pyrometer indicates the temperature at the crown—or highest part—of the balloon. Without a pyrometer it is possible to build up more heat in the balloon bag than it can safely withstand.

The heart of the balloon is the burner. It is usually suspended over the pilot's head and controlled by means of a hand valve.

Finally, we have the component known as the envelope, the hot air container which is not exactly a balloon in that it is open at the throat at all times. "Balloon" in this case is a term which refers to the complete apparatus. The envelope is usually made of high-strength, heat-resistant, rip-stop nylon, and it is fastened to the basket by means of heat resistant steel cables. The envelope is sometimes coated internally with a plastic material which helps contain heat. One manufacturer recently tested the heat resistance of his nylon envelope by heating the air in it to 250 degrees for a period of 250 hours without any degradation of the fabric.

Like other aircraft, balloons must have an Airworthiness Certificate issued by the Federal Aviation Administration. This requires inspection from a certificated mechanic every 100 hours (or annually). In addition, an aircraft log showing inspections and repairs must be carried in the balloon at all times.

Some-built balloons, which make up about 15 per cent of those aerostats currently flying, are not subject to these requirements. During construction, however, they must be monitored by an FAA inspector who will also determine the frequency of inspection required for the completed aircraft in order for it to be airworthy. The inspector may also impose on its operation certain limitations that he feels necessary for safety.

All required inspections must be carried out by an FAA certified aircraft mechanic or by a designee at an FAA-approved repair station. He will inspect the envelope for possible heat damage and test the fabric for strength, tears, abrasions and seam

The absence of storage space . . . makes it essential that equipment be stowed carefully. . .

separations. The cables will be checked for burns, abrasions or excessive wear. Vents will be examined carefully, as well as the condition of the Velcro on certain balloons, or the metal pins and fittings on others. The burner system will be checked for leaks, proper pressure and ignition. The color of the flame will indicate whether a proper mixture of fuel and atmospheric gases is taking place. The basket or gondola will be inspected for structural integrity.

As with other certificated aircraft, the pilot or owner can legally perform only preventative maintenance on his balloon. Normally this is limited to such minor repairs of fabric as stitching a patch cloth over a hole or tear.

Following each flight, the pilot should check the vents to make certain they are not choked with bits of grass, dirt or other debris accumulated in landing or launching. These should be secured and made ready for the next flight.

After the flight, the envelope is usually folded and placed in a cloth or canvas bag which fits into the basket for easier carrying. The balloon should be stored only in a cool dry place to avoid mildew. The storage area should be free of rats or mice, both of which sometimes enjoy nibbling at the fabric or wicker.

Finally, special care should be taken in the storage of fuel tanks, even when they are considered empty, since there is always

After flight, the envelope is folded and stored. It is also an excellent time to inspect the envelope.

Bill Huddy

some residual propane present. A basement or garage is definitely not recommended. Propane leaks are always a possibility and the propane can be ignited by any household equipment with an open flame (such as a water heater, clothes dryer or furnace). The lifting power of propane has been well established. There is no need to test it with your home.

ANNUAL INSPECTION AND REPAIRS

A type certificated balloon must be inspected annually (every 100 hours for commercially-used balloons) by an FAA-certified repair station, the manufacturer, or an A&P (airframe and power-plant) mechanic experienced with that make of balloon. Inspections usually cost from $100 to $200. Repairs to balloons must be performed by FAA-certified personnel, and home repairs or repairs by uncertified persons may invalidate the airworthiness certificate and owner's insurance.

Although modern hot air ballooning is a relatively young sport, the equipment, rigging and accessories are extremely reliable. Nevertheless, the same careful attention is essential to safe flying in balloons as it is with any aircraft. Balloons are perhaps the most "forgiving" of all aircraft, but they are not free of design defects, wear, deterioration and accidental damage, and thus do require regular inspections, maintenance and repair.

There are three basic causes of hot air balloon damage: improper inflation, approaches and landings made in unfamiliar or unpredictable places, and the fact that balloons are not yet perfected in design.

Inflation Damage

Damage due to poor inflation technique is usually confined to holes melted in the mouth and skirt. It rarely is severe enough to make the balloon unairworthy, unless the supporting load tapes are also damaged. Mouth and skirt damage (extending perhaps 10 feet up into the envelope) are usually repaired for cosmetic reasons by patching the melted areas. Since skirt and mouth damage is usually not structural, the patch work need not be done by a certified repairman. As a preventative measure, pilots are increasingly using auxiliary hand burners for inflations, since the cost of the burner is easily offset by savings in repairs.

Landing Damage

Damage from landings or touch and go's can be serious and extensive, but it is usually quite visible to the pilot, and is apt to be repaired promptly.

Damage from Improper Repair and Maintenance

A common problem in ballooning is inadequate inspection. Until 1972 this procedure could only be done by experienced and qualified inspectors/repairmen or by the balloon manufacturer. The cost to ship a balloon to the manufacturer deterred many balloonists from obtaining an adequate inspection. Pilots often made their own inspections and paid an A&P mechanic to

A common problem . . . is inadequate inspection.

Avian Balloon Works

Wicker is the traditional material for gondolas. Even pilots with a modern aluminum basket sometimes trim their gondola with wicker.

sign the log book, and too often the envelope was the only part inspected. This practice continues even today. Coupled with a variety of illegal modifications of the balloon system itself, this renders the pilot liable in the event of an accident. All but the most minor repairs *must* be made in the approved manner and meet FAA standards.

Incomplete or cursory inspections result in failures to detect worn out Velcro, faulty or worn out regulator diaphragms, frayed control lines, inaccurate instruments, worn and damaged propane fittings or hoses, and dangerously weak fabric.

Damage from improper repairs increases at a geometric rate. When a patch is made with improper fabric or thread, stresses will cause the older fabric to rip in other places. And replacing Velcro in crowns without giving equal attention to the rest of the envelope can result in a balloon that is not airworthy.

Some problems cannot be detected even under the best inspection procedures. If the balloon has a manufacturing defect which can only be detected in flight, standard inspection procedures (which do not include a check flight) will not catch the problems. Many are evident only when balloons are test-flown before delivery. Others appear only after the parts involved are broken in.

Tanks and Fuel Systems

A number of problems involve water in the fuel system, often because the tanks were not treated with methanol. Instances of broken dip tubes have caused a reduction in heat output during flight, which could result in serious or fatal landings. Quick-release valves for propane tanks have been activated in flight, causing injuries to passengers and pilot, and faulty check valves on a propane tank have occasionally meant landing on vapor. Tanks have been found with faulty gauges, improperly installed valves and leaking fittings. Home-designed and installed fittings have resulted in leaks and occasionally in fires.

All of these problems can go undetected unless detailed inspections are made at frequent intervals.

Burners

A common accident with serious results involves unprotected burner fittings. Cables from the envelope to the basket often wrap around burner fittings and break pieces of the stainless steel tubing, causing liquid propane to shoot up into the envelope or down into the basket.

Burners are the power plant of the aircraft and deserve special attention and regular inspection before and after every flight.

Repair Procedures

As mentioned before, all repairs of structural damage or the replacement of fabric, tapes, seams, cables, or fittings require supervision of an FAA-certificated A&P mechanic or the original manufacturer. Appropriate entries must be made in the logbook and duly signed off before that equipment can be used for flight.

Envelope

Small tears not exceeding two inches in length can be spliced with three-inch-wide tape, applied to both the inside and outside of the bag. If this repair is within 15 feet of the mouth, however, the tape must be sewn with one stitch around the tear and one around the perimeter of the tape.

Large tears in one direction can be lap-spliced with new material, but large tears in two directions are best repaired by a one-inch lap patch. Patching can be expedited by using a one-inch, two-sided tape to hold the new material in place for sewing.

Burn holes in excess of one inch in diameter require patching with new material. Singed and melted globs must be trimmed before sewing.

Load tape repairs require lap-splicing of ends with new material of equal or greater strength. They must be sewn with no less than six stitches for a distance of not less than eight inches on both ends (minimum tape length is 16 inches).

Any damage effecting the structural integrity of the envelope *must* terminate flight operations. It is the duty of all crew members to inform the pilot of all damage. Final responsibility, however, rests with the PIC.

A common accident with serious results involves unprotected burner fittings.

Jack Stewart

The skirt must be removed . . . if more than one burn hole exceeds 10 inches.

Skirt

Immediate repair of any skirt damage is encouraged. Edges of tears or burn holes exposed to the flame can increase in severity. Immediate repair is not critical unless damage exceeds three tears (or wire burns) less than 16 inches in total length, or if the burn holes exceed 10 inches in diameter. The skirt must be removed at the end of the flying period if more than one burn hole exceeds eight inches in diameter, if one burn hole exceeds 10 inches, if any burn hole severs a double-stitch seam or if any Velcro or structural tape is burned.

Straight tears or wire burns can be repaired by using two-inch-wide tape. Sew around the tape and tear edge.

Burn Holes

Burn holes can be repaired as follows: lay the effected panel on a plywood surface, pinning its edges to maintain the panel's original shape according to the pattern provided. Cut all melted edges that might break the sewing needle. Be careful not to cut closer than one inch to seams, ring holder or scallop tape. Open the scallop tape or ring holder seam if the fabric is burned closer than one inch (or replace the tape or seam with new parts if they are burned also).

Ink the patch area with a marking pen, following the natural lines of the existing tape and stitching. Tape along this line with a ¾-inch strip of double-sided tape. Overlay the patch to the taped area and sew it with a double stitch. If a double-stitch seam of an existing panel edge has been covered, re-sew it using an extra strip of new material so the panel shape can be maintained. If in doubt about the best repair procedures, contact the manufacturer.

FEDERAL AVIATION REGULATIONS

Keep in mind that certain procedures must be followed whenever repairs or alterations are made to the balloon. Part 43.13 (A and B) of the FARs states: *Each person maintaining or altering . . . shall use methods, techniques and practices acceptable to the Administrator. He shall use the tools, equipment and test apparatus necessary to assure completion of the work in accordance with accepted industry practices. If special equipment or test apparatus is recommended by the manufacturer . . . he must use that equipment or apparatus or its equivalent . . . and each person maintaining or altering or performing preventative maintenance shall do that work in such a manner, and use materials of such a quality that the condition of the aircraft . . . or appliance worked on will be at least equal to its original or properly altered condition (with regard to aerodynamic function, structural strength, resistance to vibration and deterioration and other qualities affecting airworthiness.)*

BALLOON SAFETY
6

Safe flying is no accident. All balloon flights are conducted in compliance with FAA Regulations, which were formulated to prevent unnecessary risks. Fliers' adherence to the regulations has made balloon flight the safest aerial activity within the jurisdiction of the FAA.

Throughout this book, safety suggestions have been woven into the text, because it is impossible to talk about ballooning without mentioning safety in the same breath. In this chapter, we will crystallize each of the safety measures mentioned earlier.

There are recent-experience requirements for all pilots. At least two hours in the preceding 30 days is considered a minimum for carrying passengers or giving instruction.

All cross-country flights by students must be approved by an instructor prior to the flight. On student flights, a commercial pilot or instructor is on location and in full charge of all operations. A student pilot owning his own balloon is still under the jurisdiction of the commercial pilot on location.

The instructor or commercial pilot can abort a student flight when unsafe conditions exist, when FAA Regulations are being violated or when the conduct of the student warrants grounding. It is the responsibility of the instructor or commercial pilot on location to report to the FAA Safety Officer all violations and unsafe practices of balloonists, both student pilots and private or commercial pilots.

All balloons will carry as standard equipment a non-conductive handling line at least 150 feet long and of 3000-pound test. However, drag lines are not considered safe at any time. (Hemp and nylon are both electrical conductors when contacting 600 volts or more.)

No flights will be made when surface winds exceed 10 m.p.h. Maximum flight duration will not exceed 90 per cent of fuel-time. And free flight will end 15 minutes prior to sunset unless the balloon is equipped with regulation navigation lights.

All flights will be made within the safety limitations of the balloon (e.g. envelope temperature, payload and ambient tem-

Taking off adjacent to power lines is a risky business at best. In this series of photos, only a hasty spot landing averted disaster.

perature). At no time shall a balloon be loaded to exceed the manufacturer's specification.

It is advisable to maintain radio contact with the chase vehicle, and two methods of ignition should always be on board (e.g. lighter, matches, striker).

Changing fuel tanks or lines in flight should not be attempted. Land, stabilize the balloon and then change.

Tethered balloon flights have additional safety considerations. Since a tethered balloon is potentially a free balloon, all of the free-balloon suggestions should be observed. Striker-igniters and associated equipment should be on board. Before inflation the ground crew should be briefed on the possibility of a free flight. The same preflight procedures and checking should precede each tethered flight, just as it does each free flight.

Tether flights should be attempted only on calm days and in safe locations. An area of at least 200 square feet is needed, and it should have a clear span and be free of obstacles. Having a reliable wind measuring gauge at the tether site is recommended. Watch closely for increasing wind velocity.

Tethered balloons should be moored with a 3000-pound test line, preferably of half-inch nylon rope. Three or four tether lines should be anchored to solid objects. Steel cable is not a recommended tether, because it has little stretch before failure, and is not easily handled.

A tripod (three-rope) tether is most effective if the ropes are evenly spaced, two ropes upwind and one downwind. They should be tied off, allowing equal length for each rope and for the basket to be positioned in the center. If this is not possible before inflation, it should be done as soon as the balloon is upright.

In a small area, no tether balloon should be inflated before ropes are tied to it and to anchor points. They may be tied off and lengthened after the balloon is upright. The red deflation line should be tied separately to a fixed object.

One crew member should be assigned to each tether line, and he should stay at his position until relieved or re-assigned. Wind can come up suddenly and it is important for every crew member to be where he is most needed.

Tethering is most successful when crew members work each line from the end nearest its anchor point, always keeping the line taut. Gloves should be worn to prevent rope burns. Spectators should be prevented from going underneath the balloon, and kept away from the handling and tether ropes. A private or commercial balloon pilot will be the PIC of all tethered flights. Student pilots may not take passengers aloft. Students cannot log tethered time as flight time leading to an LTA Free Balloon Rating.

The payload for a given balloon shall not exceed the manufacturer's recommended or certified load, and the number of passengers shall not exceed the manufacturer's recommendation or

the maximum gross weight allowable for ambient temperature. A tethered balloon shall not be flown without a calibrated, functioning temperature gauge, and at no time shall the maximum envelope temperature be exceeded. A tethered balloon should not be tossed into the air by its ground crew.

All tethered flights will be conducted in accordance with Part 101 of the FAA regulations. Flights should be terminated when the PIC feels that unsafe conditions exist.

POWER LINES

There are few real hazards in balloon flying, but of those that do exist, lines are the most dangerous. During the past few years, there have been several accidents involving power lines. Almost every one has resulted in serious injury or loss of life. In all cases they have been the result of poor judgment—pilot error.

Power lines are lethal, and it is important for pilots to observe certain cautions. There are three situations in which power lines must be considered: during take offs, while flying low and during landings.

Most pilots have experienced the common problem of a burner going out and not re-igniting. No pilot consciously approaches power lines at low altitude. Instead of believing that flying conditions are stable or improving, assume the worst. By doing so, you diminish the likelihood of contacting power lines.

Take offs

Several recent fatalities have involved ascents upwind in close proximity to power lines. In an upwind situation one option is to have sufficient buoyancy to assure a rapid rate of ascent to clear downwind obstacles, but there are limitations to this practice.

Fifty to 60 pounds of positive buoyancy would seem sufficient to make a straight-up ascent. This presumes, however, a wind condition above similar to that on the surface. But it is not uncommon to have a faster-moving layer of air blowing over the tree tops and surrounding terrain.

Even with positive buoyancy, two things happen at lift off, usually simultaneously. As the envelope enters the layer of moving air, the balloon starts moving with the air in the direction of downwind power lines. In addition to the total weight of the balloon and passengers, there are some two tons of air inside the envelope. With this inertia the balloon will not stop or start instantly. Consequently, there is a definite time lag before the balloon becomes displaced in the new layer of air. This means the layer of air is moving much faster than the balloon, resulting in a relative wind which rapidly cools the envelope and lessens the rate of climb. Even with the blast valve on full to compensate for this cooling trend, little response is obtained until the balloon is moving at the speed of the wind. By this time the balloon may already be into the power lines.

Orville Andrews

A tethered balloon is potentially a free balloon, so all the safety regulations should still be adhered to. For example, no tethered balloon should lift off without a properly functioning temperature gauge.

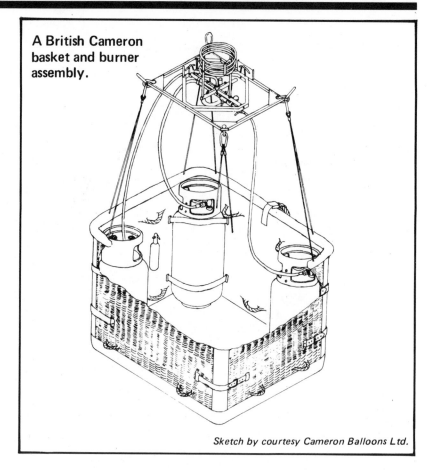

A British Cameron basket and burner assembly.

Sketch by courtesy Cameron Balloons Ltd.

Consider the possible situation of a take off adjacent to a power line. What is known about the flight conditions that will effect the performance of the balloon?

The pilot does not have many specific facts available at lift off. The wind direction may well be the only external condition he knows about and this can quickly change into an unknown. The gross weight, surface wind speed, upper wind speed and direction, outside temperature and humidity and the thermal activity are all important conditions. But in this case, the pilot is forced to substitiute educated guesses for absolute facts. A little distrust goes a long way. "In balloons we must sometimes distrust " should be a motto concerning power lines.

On most flights we can operate safely with reasonable guesses. Even when we make bad guesses, the consequences are not critical. Strategy when approaching a power line, however, must be based on complete *distrust* of the balloon's performance.

Let's assume the balloon will not ascend at a speed greater than 50 feet per minute. Further, we can assume the minimum altitude for a safe crossing over a power line is 200 feet. Under these circumstances, the minimum safe horizontal distance from a power line for launching will be: 176 feet with a wind speed of two m.p.h., and 352 feet with a four m.p.h. wind. At six m.p.h., the minimum horizontal distance is 528 feet, and at eight m.p.h. it is 704 feet.

Again, these figures are only guesses. To allow for error, pick out a significant mark halfway to the power lines. If the balloon has not achieved a minimum of 100 feet above the surface, rip the deflation line. Set a limit and if this is not achieved immediately, rip!

Low Level Flying

Low level (contour) flying presents many opportunities in which a balloon may be in close proximity to power lines. Obviously, flying at 1000 feet presents no problem, but a great deal of fun-flying and all landing approaches are done at low altitude.

There are three factors that can rapidly change the altitude of a balloon in equilibrium while crossing over power lines. The one most prevalent is a low altitude wind shear, a common condition during the midday when cumulus clouds are in the area. This presents a situation in which the balloon is traveling in one direction and encounters another layer of air moving at a different speed or in a different direction. This causes a rapid cooling of the envelope which can start an unanticipated rate of descent.

Radios are not required for normal flights, but they are ideal for keeping in touch with the chase crew.

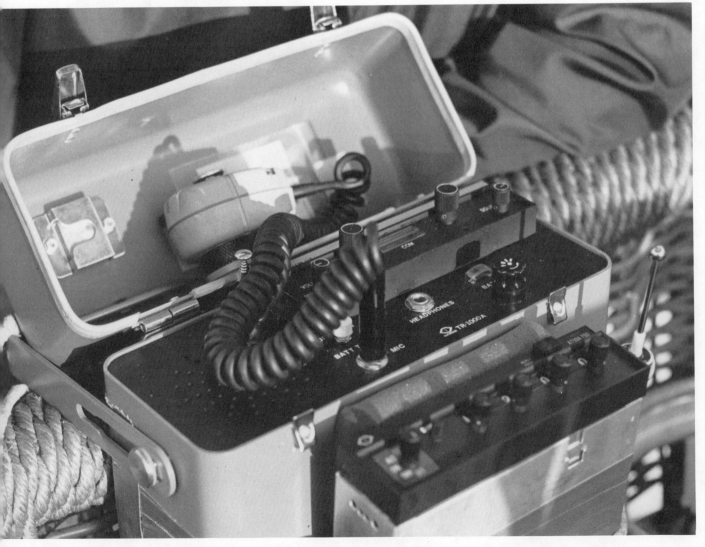

Karl Muszar

If the balloon has not reached 100 feet, rip the deflation line.

As a rule of thumb, a breeze felt on the face or neck is an indication that the balloon is encountering a wind shear. An immediate opening of the blast valve is required to offset the forthcoming cooling effect.

Another hazard of low-level flying is an unexpected flame-out just prior to crossing power lines. If there have been any pilot light problems during the flight, it is good practice to have the relighter in hand when flying at low altitude. And on a warm, sunny day you are more vulnerable to the effects of ground heating at low altitude. If you've been flying over plowed fields or

rocky terrain and then pass over water or a green area prior to approaching power lines, you could be in trouble. It is good practice to keep a watchful eye on the terrain below and try to anticipate how it will effect the balloon.

The best approach to power lines is to always have the balloon at a slight rate of ascent. There is one definite guideline for crossing a power line in flight: be well above it.

Landings

During landing, problems with obstacles are frequently encountered when visibility is limited, the wind is high, or the field is small. Always assume that every road—whether paved, gravel or dirt—has power lines. Power poles—often hidden by trees and buildings—can take you by surprise. And there can often be a long span of electrical wire out to the middle of a field for the operation of a well pump or windmill. In these cases, a sharp eye and a little forethought can keep you out of a lot of trouble.

All balloon pilots want to land next to a road for easy recovery, but this usually means landing near power lines. Landings should always be made on the downwind side of a road to lessen the danger of encountering power lines in case deflation does not go as rapidly as expected. As in low-level flying, an approach to these power lines or roads should be made from a low altitude, using a slight climb when approaching the lines and then dropping in on the other side. Carrying your balloon a few feet back to the road is much better than an ambulance attendant carrying *you* back.

Emergency Procedures

A number of recent accidents have been caused by pilots waiting too long to see if they were going to get enough reaction from the blast valve. We are all aware of the time lag between action and reaction in maneuvering a balloon. It is easy to float along toward danger with the hope that at any moment your balloon will leap over the problem. Many pilots have kept up this hope right into power lines.

It makes sense to have in mind a definite cut-off distance where hope is replaced by positive action. If you are approaching a power line and your balloon has not responded, take positive action by deflating. Many balloonists seem to think that deflating at the level of the wires is a poor second choice to actually hitting them. This is definitely not so. Bend your knees and hold on. You might twist an ankle or skin an elbow, but this is preferable to the often fatal choice of running into the wires.

VELCRO

There is increasing evidence to indicate that the Velcro in balloon deflation panels must be viewed suspiciously after as little as 100 hours of service life. Pilots are well advised to look at their Velcro for evidences of deterioration.

The hooks are easily inspected with the naked eye. Hooks appear to hold up well in balloon service, probably because their

There is one guideline for crossing a power line: be well above it.

fabric is of a larger diameter than the loops. The loops (the fluffy side) tend to be more complex, but the state of fluffiness is often an indication of their strength.

As yet, there is no accepted method for testing Velcro. It is therefore suggested that the pilot occasionally peel down a sealed rip panel along its entire length to feel the strength of Velcro. If a particular section feels weak, a detailed examination should be made. A short piece of new Velcro can be used as a gauge against which to compare the old Velcro.

There is additional evidence to indicate that nylon has a tendency to shrink at temperatures common to balloons. The combination of shrunk nylon and weakened Velcro can result in the accidental opening of a rip panel. As the top shrinks away from the loose load tapes (which normally carry the balloon loads and support the fabric valve) the load is transferred from the tapes to the valve fabric. The valve fabric and Velcro fabric are not designed to be load-bearing, hence accidental rip opening should be anticipated if this condition occurs.

In a new balloon which is dimensionally correct, the Velcro loads are quite low and are normally applied to the Velcro only in a shearing plane.

A balloon will give warning of a bad rip panel condition before a serious failure occurs. Accordingly, pilots should be especially alert for inadvertent rip openings during inflation or even a tiny opening in the rip panel during flight. These symptoms suggest that the loads are being transferred from the load tapes to the rip panel fabric.

Dimensional analysis of the valve fabric and the load tapes will verify that a problem exists. The loose load tapes should be shorter than the valve fabric to insure that the load is on the tapes. Measurements must be carefully made so the observations are all in the same plane.

In balloons with a side rip panel, as opposed to a circular rip panel, it becomes extremely important that the valve fabric is as large as or larger than the valve opening. Determination of these dimensions can normally be made by measuring the adjacent gore fabric that is fixed to the load tapes.

If you suspect weak Velcro, rip it out on the ground before it rips out on you in the air.

BALLOON WEATHER

Wind, rain, sleet, snow, hail, fog, haze and smog exert important effects upon a balloon, but the pilot who is properly informed can minimize their negative factors.

It is important that you have a knowledge of local weather to supplement the predictions supplied by the Weather Bureau. This is essential because: weather does not always turn out as predicted, weather stations are often spaced far apart and weather conditions between stations can vary widely from those reported, and weather predictions are not absolute and infallable.

You need to take the information provided and relate it to your own aircraft, experience and limitations in order to determine the practicability of your proposed flight.

In planning a balloon flight, it is essential that complete weather information be obtained. This includes the surface winds and temperature at the launch site, the direction and force of winds aloft, the temperature at your proposed flight altitudes and the weather predictions for the estimated time and direction of your flight. A knowledge of these factors will determine whether the flight will be "Go" or "No-Go."

To obtain a weather briefing it is best to call a Flight Service Station or the Pilot's Automatic Weather Answering Service at least six hours prior to your launch, and again just before you start inflating. By doing so you may be able to sense a weather trend. FSS will give you the position of highs, lows, fronts, ridges and current temperatures. The force and direction of the c-wind at ground level and flight altitudes is also reported.

GETTING STARTED
7

If you've digested all the preceding information about ballooning and the inclination is still with you to become a balloon pilot, you'll need to know where to go from here.

One requirement you must get out of the way is the written examination. You can usually take this at any General Aviation District Office (GADO) or Flight Standards District Office (FSDO) of the Federal Aviation Administration. Call the local FAA tower or Flight Service Station (they are listed under "United States Government, Department of Transportation" in the white pages of your phone book). With a photographic memory of the contents of *All About Ballooning,* you should have little difficulty in passing the examination.

As far as the actual flying goes, the country abounds with balloon pilots. Whether you life in Alaska or Florida, Maine or California, someone nearby has a balloon and will be glad to get you started. Only in Hawaii is ballooning a no-no.

Your local FAA office can usually help locate a balloonist, or you might try the yellow pages (they're frequently listed under Balloon Instruction or Balloon Schools). If this doesn't yield results, drop a note to the Balloon Federation of America (Suite 610, 806 Fifteenth Street Northwest, Washington, D.C. 20005) for the names of balloonists in your area. If you live anywhere in Europe, you can obtain similar information by writing the

British Balloon and Airship Club, 75 Victoria Street, London SW1.

When you locate a balloonist, get in touch and hitch a ride. If you decide after a flight or two that ballooning is the best thing since popcorn, there are several ways to proceed. The cost will depend on how you wish to participate.

First join an existing club if there's one near you. You'll then have access to the club balloons and facilities. Membership costs vary from club to club, but they are usually in the $300-$650 range with monthly dues of about $10. New clubs are springing up every day. Some of the well-known clubs include:

Albuquerque Aerostat Ascension Association, 3323 Princeton NE, Albuquerque, NM 87107.

Arizona Balloon Club, 505 West Camelback, Suite 200, Phoenix, AZ 85013.

Balloonatics Balloon Club, 2345 Walnut, Denver, CO 80205.

Gateway Aerostatic Association, 12557B Western Cape, St. Louis, MO 63341.

LERC Wind Drifters, 2814 Empire Avenue, Burbank, CA 91503.

Lockheed Balloon Club, Box 504, Sunnyvale, CA 94088.

Westwinds Balloon Club, Box 897, Tustin, CA 92680.

A second possibility is to buy your own balloon. A new one with ground support equipment will cost between $5000-$7500, more if you want top-of-the-line equipment. When you buy a balloon from a manufacturer, you'll have the fun of designing your own envelope. Flight instruction through your private pilot rating is usually included in the cost.

Manufacturers of FAA type-certified balloons from whom literature and descriptive material is available include:

Mike Adams Balloon Loft, Box 12168, Atlanta, GA 30305.

The Balloon Works, Rhyne Aerodrome, RFD 2, Statesville, NC 28677.

Cameron Balloons US, 3600 Elizabeth Road, Ann Arbor, MI 48103.

Don Piccard Balloons, Box 1902, Newport Beach, CA 92663.

Raven Industries, Box 1007, Sioux Falls, SD 57101.

Semco Balloons, Route 3, Box 514, Aerodrome Way, Griffing, GA 30223.

Thunder Balloons America, 11 Eagle Nest NE, Albuquerque, NM 87112.

Another idea is to get together with a group of friends and start your own club. Obtain catalogs and prices from manufacturers, and contact a local instructor or manufacturer's representative for flight instruction. Buy a balloon and split the cost among yourselves. Remember that ballooning is a group activity and by sharing expenses you will have a readily available ground and chase crew.

If you decide to build your own balloon, you can get up-to-date information from Hare Balloons, 1056 Laguna Avenue, Los Angeles, CA 90026 or from Balloon and Airship Constructors, 3217 North Delta, Rosemead, CA 91770.

Finally, you can enroll in an FAA-approved balloon school. The cost of earning a private pilot rating runs from $900-$1500. It takes a minimum of three weeks and includes ground school, use of a balloon and instruction. Among the leading balloon schools are the following:

Aerie Balloon Enterprises, 4040 South 28th, Arlington, VA 22206.

Alberta (Canada) Free Balloonist Society, 1712 Home Road NW, Calgary 45, Alberta, Canada 73B 1G9.

. . . by sharing expenses you will have a readily available ground and chase crew.

Balloon Ascensions, Route 11, Box 279, Statesville, NC 28677.

Balloon Excelsior, 777 Beechwood Drive, Daly City, CA 94015.

The Balloon Port, 9901 Conway Road, St. Louis, MO 63124.

The Balloon Port, RFD 2, Statesville, NC 28677.

Highamerica Balloon Center, 2545 Leach Road, Auburn Heights, MI 48057.

Dan Hacker, 4451 Tanglewood Way, Napa, CA 94558.

Nevermore Balloon Sales, 1307 Lee Lane, Sykesville, MD 21784.

Ray Gallagher Enterprises, 407 Fullerton, Newport Beach, CA 92663.

Scorpion Productions, 246 Lomita Drive, Perris, CA 92370.

Sky Promotions, 20 Nassau Street, Princeton, NJ 08540.

Sky Rider Balloon Port, Lake Placid, FL 33852.

Truckee Balloon Works, Box 2456, Olympic Valley, CA 95730.

Wiederkehr Balloon Academy, 1604 Euclid, St. Paul, MN 55106.

World Balloon Championships, 3323 Princeton N.E., Albuquerque, NM.

The reward of flying silently over a world below . . .

Getting a balloon rating isn't difficult and requires no special or unique skills. However, it does require study (read AAB again and again), patience (wind and weather are usually unpredictable and uncooperative), fortitude (or is getting up at 4:00 a.m. your usual lifestyle?) and hard work (bouncing in the chase truck over impossible terrain, carting tanks, and lugging the basket around). The reward of flying silently over a world below, however, is enough to make everything else fade into inconsequentiality.

When calling for weather information, you need to tell the weather briefer the following: whether you're a student, private or commercial pilot, the aircraft you will be flying (hot air balloon, number and color), your estimated time and place of launch, your projected time aloft and (fingers crossed) your direction of flight. In flight you can also receive specific weather conditions by tuning your radio to the given weather frequency.

Remember that weather forecasts are general in nature. They often vary from conditions at your launch area. It is easy to fall into the trap of disbelieving the forecast because launch site weather differs from the prediction. You don't fly a balloon at your launch site. You fly it at altitudes and in areas for which forecasts are usually accurate.

Reading the weather is not a skill a balloon pilot learns overnight. Achieving a measure of skill at it includes learning to read a station (weather) map with its storehouse of information and mysterious symbols. One must also recognize cloud formations and air movements, as well as know the effects of rain, hail and snow on your balloon and how icing (even on warm days) can effect your burners and your altitude.

Understanding the weather is one key to a long and successful balloon flight, and it begins before you call for weather information. Knowledge about weather can only be gained by thoroughly studying it.

The standard weather reference is *Aviation Weather* (AC-00-6A), available from the Superintendent of Documents, GPO, Washington, DC 20402. A companion volume, *Aviation Weather Services* (AC-00-45), augments the information in *Aviation Weather*. Other excellent sources are the FAA's *Airman's Information Manual* and Sanderson's *Aviation Fundamentals* and *Aviation Weather*.

Definite minimum weather conditions exist for all balloon flights.

Ceiling:

A minimum of 2000 feet Mean Sea Level (MSL) for flights in control areas when maximum altitude will not exceed 500 feet Above Ground Level (AGL) during the training flight. A minimum of 7000 feet MSL will be maintained when flights to 5000 feet AGL will be conducted. A transponder will be carried on all flights above 3000 feet MSL.

Visibility:

A minimum of three miles inside Control Zones, and a minimum of one mile in control areas when flights remain below 500 feet AGL.

Dew Point:

The spread must be two degrees or better.

Surface Winds:

All surface wind measurements will be taken at the launch site, and they should not exceed eight m.p.h., the maximum for high-wind inflation and demonstrations.

Winds Aloft:

For 3000-5000-foot flights, the winds aloft should not exceed exceed 30 m.p.h.

Thermal Conditions:

No thermal conditions shall exist when student pilots are in solo flight.

Hazardous Weather:

No hazardous weather shall exist within 50 miles upwind from the launch site. It is a pilot's responsibility to search every known weather source to assure that the balloon flight will be safe from unexpected weather conditions.

Surface Conditions:

The surface or ground shall be reasonably dry or in such a condition that the envelope will not get wet.

Dangerous Conditions For Ballooning:

These conditions are gusty winds, thermal conditions, dead calm air, thunderstorms in the area (or predicted), strong winds of 35 m.p.h. or more at 2000 feet AGL and sudden shifts in wind direction.

It is said that there are old pilots and there are bold pilots, but that there are no old, bold pilots. If you desire to vie with me for the distinction of being the world's oldest aeronaut, your longevity will depend mostly on the weather and your reaction to it.

FAA REGULATIONS 8

61.3   Requirements for certificates, rating, and authorizations.

(a) *Pilot certificate.* No person may act as pilot in command or in any other capacity as a required pilot flight crewmember of a civil aircraft of United States registry unless he has in his personal possession a current pilot certificate issued to him under this Part. However, when the aircraft is operated within a foreign country a current pilot license issued by the country in which the aircraft is operated may be used.

(b) *Pilot certificate: foreign aircraft.* No person may, within the United States, act as pilot in command or in any other capacity as a required pilot flight crewmember of a civil aircraft of foreign registry unless he has in his personal possession a current pilot certificate issued to him under this Part, or a pilot license issued to him or validated for him by the country in which the aircraft is registered.

(c) *Medical certificate.* Except for free balloon pilots piloting balloons and glider pilots piloting gliders, no person may act as pilot in command or in any other capacity as a required pilot flight crewmember of an aircraft under a certificate issued to him under this Part, unless he has in his personal possession an appropriate current medical certificate issued under Part 67 of this chapter.

(d) *Flight instructor certificate.* Except for lighter-than-air flight instruction in lighter-than-air aircraft, and for instruction in air transportation service given by the holder of an Airline Transport Pilot Certificate under 61.169, no person other than the holder of a flight instructor certificate issued by the Ad-ministrator with an appropriate rating on that certificate may—

(1) Give any of the flight instruction required to qualify for a solo flight, solo cross-country flight, or for the issue of a pilot or flight instructor certificate or rating;

(2) Endorse a pilot logbook to show that he has given any flight instruction; or

(3) Endorse a student pilot certificate or logbook for solo operating privileges.

(h) *Inspection of certificate.* Each person who holds a pilot certificate, flight instructor certificate, medical certificate, authorization, or license required by this Part shall present it for inspection upon the request of the Administrator, an authorized representative of the National Transportation Safety Board, or any Federal, State, or local law enforcement officer.

61.5   Certificates and ratings issued under this Part.

(a) The following certificates are issued under this Part:

(1) Pilots certificates:

(i) Student pilot.

(ii) Private pilot.

(iii) Commercial pilot.

(iv) Airline transport pilot.

(2) Flight instructor certificates.

(b) The following ratings are placed on pilot certificates (other than student pilot) where applicable:

(1) Aircraft category ratings:

(i) Airplane.

(ii) Rotorcraft.

(iii) Glider.

(iv) Lighter-than-air.

(4) Lighter-than-air class ratings:

(i) Airship.

(ii) Free balloon.

61.7 Obsolete certificates and ratings.

(a) The holder of a free balloon pilot certificate issued before November 1, 1973, may not exercise the privileges of that certificate.

(b) The holder of a pilot certificate that bears any of the following category ratings without an associated class rating, may not exercise the privileges of that category rating:

(1) Rotorcraft.

(2) Lighter-than-air.

(3) Helicopter.

(4) Autogiro.

61.9 Exchange of obsolete certificates and ratings for current certificates and ratings.

(a) The holder of an unexpired free balloon pilot certificate, or an unexpired pilot certificate with an obsolete category rating listed in 61.7 (b) of this Part may exchange that certificate for a certificate with the following applicable category and class rating, without a further showing of competency, until October 31, 1975. After that date, a free balloon pilot certificate or certificate with an obsolete rating expires.

(f) *Free balloon pilot certificate.* The holder of a free balloon pilot certificate is issued a commercial pilot certificate with a lighter-than-air category rating and, if appropriate, with the limitations provided in 61.141 of this Part.

(g) *Lighter-than-air pilot certificate or pilot certificate with lighter-than-air category (without a class rating).*

(1) In the case of an application made before November 1, 1975, the holder of a lighter-than-air pilot certificate or a pilot certificate with a lighter-than-air category rating (without a class rating) is issued a private or commercial pilot certificate, as appropriate, with a lighter-than-air category rating and airship and free balloon class ratings.

(2) In the case of an application made after October 31, 1975, the holder of a lighter-than-air pilot

certificate with an airship rating issued prior to November 1, 1973, may be issued a free balloon class rating upon passing the appropriate flight test in a free balloon.

61.11 Expired pilot certificates and reissuance.

(a) No person who holds an expired pilot certificate or rating may exercise the privileges of that pilot certificate, or rating.

(b) Except as provided, the following certificates and ratings have expired and are not reissued:

(2) A private or commercial pilot certificate, or a lighter-than-air or free balloon pilot certificate, issued before July 1, 1945. However, each of those certificates issued after June 30, 1945, and bearing an expiration date, may be reissued without an expiration date.

61.13 Application and qualification.

(a) Application for a certificate and rating, or for an additional rating under this Part is made on a form and in a manner prescribed by the Administrator.

(f) Unless authorized by the Administrator—

(1) A person whose pilot certificate is suspended may not apply for any pilot or flight instructor certificate or rating during the period of suspension; and

(2) A person whose flight instructor certificate only is suspended may not apply for any rating to be added to that certificate during the period of suspension.

(g) Unless the order of revocation provides otherwise—

(1) A person whose pilot certificate is revoked may not apply for any pilot or flight instructor certificate or rating for one year after the date of revocation; and

(2) A person whose flight instructor certificate only is revoked may not apply for any flight instructor certificate for one year after the date of revocation.

61.17 Temporary certificate.

(1) A temporary pilot or flight instructor certificate, or a rating, effective for a period of not more than 90 days, is issued to a qualified applicant pending a review of his qualifications and the issuance of a

permanent certificate or rating by the Administrator. The permanent certificate or rating is issued to an applicant found qualified and a denial thereof is issued to an applicant found not qualified.

(b) A temporary certificate issued under paragraph (a) of this section expires—

(1) At the end of the expiration date stated thereon; or

(2) Upon receipt by the applicant of—

(i) The certificate or rating sought; or

(ii) Notice that the certificate or rating sought is denied.

61.19   Duration of pilot and flight instructor certificates.

(a) *General.* The holder of a certificate with an expiration date may not, after that date, exercise the privileges of that certificate.

(b) *Student pilot certificate.* A student pilot certificate expires at the end of the 24th month after the month in which it is issued.

(c) *Other pilot certificates.* Any pilot certificate (other than a student pilot certificate) issued under this Part is issued without a specific expiration date. However, the holder of a pilot certificate issued on the basis of a foreign pilot license may exercise the privileges of that certificate only while the foreign pilot license on which that certificate is based is effective.

(d) *Flight instructor certificate.* A flight instructor certificate—

(1) Is effective only while the holder has a current pilot certificate and a medical certificate appropriate to the pilot privileges being exercised; and

(2) Expires at the end of the 24th month after the month in which it was last issued or renewed.

(e) *Surrender, suspension, or revocation.* Any pilot certificate or flight instructor certificate issued under this Part ceases to be effective if it is surrendered, suspended, or revoked.

(f) *Return of certificate.* The holder of any certificate issued under this Part that is suspended or revoked shall, upon the Administrator's request, return it to the Administrator.

61.23   Duration of medical certificates.

(a) A first-class medical certificate expires at the end of the last day of—

(1) The sixth month after the month of the date of examination shown on the certificate, for operations requiring an airline transport pilot certificate;

(2) The 12th month after the month of the date of examination shown on the certificate, for operations requiring only a commercial pilot certificate, and

(3) The 24th month after the month of the date of examination shown on the certificate, for operations requiring only a private or student pilot certificate.

(b) A second-class medical certificate expires at the end of the last day of—

(1) The 12th month after the month of the date of examination shown on the certificate, for operations requiring a commercial pilot certificate; and

(2) The 24th month after the month of the date of examination shown on the certificate, for operations requiring only a private or student pilot certificate.

(c) A third-class medical certificate expires at the end of the last day of the 24th month after the month of the date of examination shown on the certificate, for operations requiring a private or student pilot certificate.

61.29   Replacement of lost or destroyed certificate.

(a) An application for the replacement of a lost or destroyed airman certificate issued under this Part is made by letter to the Department of Transportation, Federal Aviation Administration, Airman Certification Branch, P.O. Box 25082, Oklahoma City, Oklahoma 73125. The letter must—

(1) State the name of the person to whom the certificate was issued, the permanent mailing address (including zip code), social security number (if any), date and place of birth of the certificate holder, and any available information regarding the grade, number, and date of issue of the certificate, and the ratings on it; and

(2) Be accompanied by a check or money order for $2.00, payable to the Federal Aviation Administration.

(b) An application for the replacement of a lost or destroyed medical certificate is made by letter to the Department of Transportation, Federal Aviation Administration, Aeromedical Certification Branch, P.O.

Box 25082, Oklahoma City, Oklahoma 73125, accompanied by a check or money order for $2.00.

(c) A person who has lost a certificate issued under this Part, or a medical certificate issued under Part 67 of this chapter, or both, may obtain a telegram from the FAA confirming that it was issued. The telegram may be carried as a certificate for a period not to exceed 60 days pending his receipt of a duplicate certificate under paragraph (a) or (b) of this section,

unless he has been notified that the certificate has been suspended or revoked. The request for such a telegram may be made by letter or prepaid telegram, including the date upon which a duplicate certificate was previously requested, if a request had been made, and a money order for the cost of the duplicate certificate. The request for a telegraphic certificate is sent to the office listed in paragraph (a) or (b) of this section, as appropriate. However, a request for both airman and medical certificates at the same time must be sent to the office prescribed in paragraph (a) of this section.

61.31 General limitations.

(a) *Type ratings required.* A person may not act as pilot in command of any of the following aircraft unless he holds a type rating for that aircraft:

(1) A large aircraft (except lighter-than-air).

(2) A helicopter, for operations requiring an airline transport pilot certificate.

(3) A turbojet powered airplane.

(4) Other aircraft specified by the Administrator through aircraft type certificate procedures.

(f) *Exception.* This section does not require a class rating for gliders, or category and class ratings for aircraft that are not type certified as airplanes, rotorcraft, or lighter-than-air aircraft. In addition, the rating limitations of this section do not apply to—

(4) The holder of a pilot certificate with a lighter-than-air category rating when operating a hot air balloon without an airborne heater.

61.39 Prerequisites for flight tests.

(a) To be eligible for a flight test for a certificate, or an aircraft or instrument rating issued under this Part, the applicant must—

(1) Have passed any required written test since the beginning of the 24th month before the month in which he takes the flight test;

(2) Have the applicable instruction and aeronautical experience prescribed in this Part;

(3) Hold a current medical certificate appropriate to the certificate he seeks or, in the case of a rating to be added to his pilot certificate, at least a third-class medical certificate issued since the beginning of the 24th month before the month in which he takes the flight test;

(4) Except for a flight test for an airline transport pilot certificate, meet the age requirement for

the issuance of the certificate or rating he seeks; and

(5) Have a written statement from an appropriately certificated flight instructor certifying that he has given the applicant flight instruction in preparation for the flight test within 60 days preceding the date of application, and finds him competent to pass the test and to have satisfactory knowledge of the subject areas in which he is shown to be deficient by his FAA airman written test report.

61.43 Flight tests: general procedures.

(a) The ability of an applicant for a private or commercial pilot certificate, or for an aircraft or instrument rating on that certificate to perform the required pilot operations is based on the following:

(1) Executing procedures and maneuvers within the aircraft's performance capabilities and limitations, including use of the aircraft's systems.

(2) Executing emergency procedures and maneuvers appropriate to the aircraft.

(3) Piloting the aircraft with smoothness and accuracy.

(4) Exercising judgment.

(5) Applying his aeronautical knowledge.

(6) Showing that he is the master of the aircraft, with the successful outcome of a procedure or maneuver never seriously in doubt.

(b) If the applicant fails any of the required pilot operations in accordance with the applicable provisions of paragraph (a) of this section, the applicant fails the flight test. The applicant is not eligible for the certificate or rating sought until he passes any pilot operations he has failed.

(c) The examiner or the applicant may discontinue the test at any time when the failure of a required pilot operation makes the applicant ineligible for the certificate or rating sought. If the test is discontinued the applicant is entitled to credit for only those entire pilot operations that he has successfully performed.

61.47 Flight tests: status of FAA inspectors and other authorized flight examiners.

An FAA inspector or other authorized flight examiner conducts the flight test of an applicant for a pilot certificate or rating for the purpose of observing the applicant's ability to perform satisfactorily the procedures and maneuvers on the flight test. The inspector or other examiner is not pilot in command of the aircraft during the flight test unless he acts in that capacity for the flight, or portion of the flight, by prior arrangement with the applicant or other person who would otherwise act as pilot in command of the flight, or portion of the flight. Notwithstanding the type of aircraft used during a flight test, the applicant and the inspector or other examiner are not, with respect to each other (or other occupants authorized by the inspector or other examiner), subject to the requirements or limitations for the carriage of passengers specified in this chapter.

61.51 Pilot logbooks.

(a) The aeronautical training and experience used to meet the requirements for a certificate or rating, or the recent flight experience requirements of this Part must be shown by a reliable record. The logging of other flight time is not required.

(b) *Logbook entries.* Each pilot shall enter the following information for each flight or lesson logged:

(1) *General.*
  (i) Date.
  (ii) Total time of flight.
  (iii) Place, or points of departure and arrival.
  (iv) Type and identification of aircraft.

(2) *Type of pilot experience or training.*
  (i) Pilot in command or solo.
  (ii) Second in command.
  (iii) Flight instruction received from an authorized flight instructor.
  (vi) Participating crew (lighter-than-air).
  (vii) Other pilot time.

(3) *Conditions of flight.*
  (i) Day or night.

(c) *Logging of pilot time.*

(1) *Solo flight time.* A pilot may log as solo flight time only that flight time when he is the sole occupant of the aircraft. However, a student pilot may also log as solo flight time that time during which he acts as the pilot in command of an airship requiring more than one flight crewmember.

(2) *Pilot-in-command flight time.*

(i) A private or commercial pilot may log as pilot in command time only that flight time during which he is the sole manipulator of the contorls of an aircraft for which he is rated,

(iii) A certificated flight instructor may log as pilot in command time all flight time during which he acts as a flight instructor.

(5) *Instruction time.* All time logged as flight instruction, instrument flight instruction, pilot ground trainer instruction, or ground instruction time must be certified by the appropriately rated and certificated instructor from whom it was received.

(d) *Presentation of logbook.*

(1) A pilot must present his logbook (or other record required by this section) for inspection upon reasonable request by the Administrator, an authorized representative of the National Transportation Safety Board, or any State or local law enforcement officer.

(2) A student pilot must carry his logbook (or other record required by this section) with him on all solo cross-country flights, as evidence of the required instructor clearances and endorsements.

61.57 Recent flight experience: pilot in command.

(a) *Flight review.* After November 1, 1974, no person may act as pilot in command of an aircraft unless, within the preceding 24 months, he has—

(1) Accomplished a flight review given to him, in an aircraft for which he is rated, by an appropriately certificated instructor or other person designated by the Administrator; and

(2) Had his log book endorsed by the person who gave him the review certifying that he has satisfactorily accomplished the flight review.

However, a person who has, within the preceding 24 months, satisfactorily completed a pilot proficiency check conducted by the FAA, an approved pilot check airman need not accomplish the flight review required by this section.

(b) *Meaning of flight review.* As used in this section, a flight review consists of—

(1) A review of the current general operating and flight rules of Part 91 of this chapter; and

(2) A review of those maneuvers and procedures which in the discretion of the person giving the review are necessary for the pilot to demonstrate that he can safely exercise the privileges of his pilot certificate.

(c) *General experience.* No person may act as pilot in command of an aircraft carrying passengers, nor of an aircraft certificated for more than one required pilot flight crewmember, unless within the preceding 90 days, he has made three takeoffs and three landings as the sole manipulator of the flight controls in an aircraft of the same category and class and, if a type rating is required, of the same type.

For the purpose of meeting the requirements of the paragraph a person may act as pilot-in-command of a flight under day VFR or day IFR if no persons or property other than as necessary for his compliance thereunder, are carried.

SUBPART C — STUDENT PILOTS

61.83 Eligibility requirements: general.

To be eligible for a student pilot certificate, a person must—

(a) Be at least 16 years of age, or at least 14 years of age for a student pilot certificate limited to the operation of a glider or free balloon;

(b) Be able to read, speak, and understand the English language, or have such operating limitations on his student pilot certificate as are necessary for the safe operation of aircraft, to be removed when he shows that he can read, speak, and understand the English language; and

(c) Hold at least a current third-class medical certificate issued under Part 67 of this chapter, or, in the case of glider or free balloon operations, certify that he has no known medical defect that makes him unable to pilot a glider or a free balloon.

61.87 Requirements for solo flight.

(a) *General.* A student pilot may not operate an aircraft in solo flight until he has complied with the requirements of this section. As used in this subpart the term solo flight means that flight time during which a student pilot is the sole occupant of the aircraft, or that flight time during which he acts as pilot in command of an airship requiring more than one flight crewmember.

(b) *Aeronautical knowledge.* He must have demonstrated to an authorized instructor that he is familiar with the flight rules of Part 91 of this chapter which are pertinent to student solo flights.

(c) *Flight proficiency training.* He must have received ground and flight instruction in at least the following procedures and operations:

  (6) *In free balloons:*

    (i) Flight preparation procedures, including preflight operations;

    (ii) Operation of hot air or gas source, ballast, valves, and rip panels, as appropriate;

    (iii) Liftoffs and climbs; and

    (iv) Descents, landings, and emergency use of rip panel (may be simulated).

Instruction must be given by an authorized flight instructor or the holder of a commercial pilot certificate with a lighter-than-air category and free balloon class rating.

(d) *Flight instructor endorsements.* A student pilot may not operate an aircraft in solo flight unless his student pilot certificate is endorsed, and unless within the preceding 90 days his pilot logbook has been endorsed, by an authorized flight instructor who—

(1) Has given him instruction in the make and model of aircraft in which the solo flight is made;

(2) Finds that he has met the requirements of this section; and

(3) Finds that he is competent to make a safe solo flight in that aircraft.

61.89 General limitations.

(a) A student pilot may not act as pilot in command of an aircraft—

(1) That is carrying a passenger;
(2) That is carrying property for compensation or hire;
(3) For compensation or hire;
(4) In furtherance of a business; or

61.91 Aircraft limitations: pilot in command.

A student pilot may not serve as pilot in command of any airship requiring more than one flight crewmember unless he has met the pertinent requirements prescribed in 61.87.

61.93 Cross-country flight requirements.

(a) *General.* A student pilot may not operate an aircraft in a solo cross-country flight, nor may he, except in emergency, make a solo flight landing at any point other than the airport of takeoff, until he meets the requirements prescribed in this section. However, an authorized flight instructor may allow a student pilot to practice solo landings and takeoffs at another airport within 25 nautical miles from the airport at which the student pilot receives instruction if he finds that the student pilot is competent to make those landings and takeoffs. As used in this section the term cross-country flight means a flight beyond a radius of 25 nautical miles from the point of takeoff.

(b) *Flight training.* A student pilot must receive instruction from an authorized instructor in at least the following pilot operations pertinent to the aircraft to be operated in a solo cross-country flight:

(5) For solo cross-country in free balloons—

(i) The use of aeronautical charts and the magnetic compass for pilotage;
(ii) The recognition of critical weather situations and the procurement and use of aeronautical weather reports and forecasts; and
(iii) Cross-country emergency procedures.

(c) *Flight instructor endorsements.* A student pilot must have the following endorsements from an authorized flight instructor:

(1) An endorsement on his student pilot certificate stating that he has received instruction in solo cross-country flying and the applicable training requirements of this section, and is competent to make cross-country solo flights in the category of aircraft involved.

(2) An endorsement in his pilot logbook that the instructor has reviewed the preflight planning and preparation for each solo cross-country flight, and he is prepared to make the flight safely under the known circumstances and the conditions listed by the instructor in the logbook. The instructor may also endorse the logbook for repeated solo cross-country flights under stipulated conditions over a course not more than 50 nautical miles from the point of departure if he has given the student flight instruction in both directions over the route, including takeoffs and landings at the airports to be used.

SUBPART D — PRIVATE PILOTS

61.103 Eligibility requirements: general.

To be eligible for a private pilot certificate, a person must—

(a) Be at least 17 years of age, except that a private pilot certificate with a free balloon or glider rating only may be issued to a qualified applicant who is at least 16 years of age;

(b) Be able to read, speak, and understand the English language, or have such operating limitations placed on his pilot certificate as are necessary for the safe operation of aircraft, to be removed when he shows that he can read, speak, and understand the English language;

(c) Hold at least a current third-class medical certificate issued under Part 67 of this chapter, or, in the case of a glider or free balloon rating, certify that he has no known medical defect that makes him unable to pilot a glider or free balloon, as appropriate;

(d) Pass a written test on the subject areas on which instruction or home study is required by 61.105;

(e) Pass an oral and flight test on procedures and maneuvers selected by an FAA inspector or examiner to determine the applicant's competency in the flight operations on which instruction is required by the flight proficiency provisions of 61.107; and

(f) Comply with the sections of this Part that apply to the rating he seeks.

61.105 Aeronautical knowledge.

An applicant for a private pilot certificate must have logged ground instruction from an authorized instructor, or must present evidence showing that he has satisfactorily completed a course of instruction or home study in at least the following areas of aeronautical knowledge appropriate to the category of aircraft for which a rating is sought.

(e) *Free balloons.*

(1) The Federal Aviation Regulations applicable to private free balloon pilot privileges, limitations, and flight operations;

(2) The use of aeronautical charts and the magnetic compass for free balloon navigation;

(3) The recognition of weather conditions of concern to the free balloon pilot, and the procurement and use of aeronautical weather reports and forecasts appropriate to free balloon operations; and

(4) Operating principles and procedures of free balloons, including gas and hot air inflation systems.

61.107 Flight proficiency.

The applicant for a private pilot certificate must have logged instruction from an authorized flight instructor in at least the following pilot operations. In addition, his logbook must contain an endorsement by an authorized flight instructor who has found him competent to perform each of those operations safely as a private pilot.

(f) *In free balloons.*

(1) Rigging and mooring;
(2) Operation of burner, if airborne heater used;
(3) Ascents and descents;
(4) Landing; and
(5) Emergencies, including the use of the ripcord (may be simulated).

61.117 Lighter-than-air rating: aeronautical experience.

An applicant for a private pilot certificate with a lighter-than-air category rating must have at least the aeronautical experience prescribed in paragraph (a) or (b) of this section, appropriate to the rating sought.

(b) *Free balloons.*

(1) If a gas balloon or hot air balloon with an airborne heater is used, a total of 10 hours in free balloons with at least 6 flights under the supervision of a person holding a commercial pilot certificate with a free balloon rating. These flights must include—

(i) Two flights, each of at least one hour's duration, if a gas balloon is used, or of 30 minutes' duration, if a hot air balloon with an airborne heater is used;

(ii) One ascent under control to 5,000 feet above the point of takeoff, if a gas balloon is used, or 3,000 feet above the point of takeoff, if a hot air balloon with an airborne heater is used; and

(iii) One solo flight in a free balloon.

(2) If a hot air balloon without an airborne heater is used, six flights in a free balloon under the supervision of a commercial balloon pilot, including at least one solo flight.

61.119 Free balloon rating: limitations.

(a) If the applicant for a free balloon rating takes his flight test in a hot air balloon with an airborne heater, his pilot certificate contains an endorsement restricting the exercise of the privilege of that rating to hot air balloons with airborne heaters. The restrictions may be deleted when the holder of the certificate obtains the pilot experience required for a rating on a gas balloon.

(b) If the applicant for a free balloon rating takes his flight test in a hot air balloon without an airborne heater, his pilot certificate contains an endorsement restricting the exercise of the privileges of that rating to hot air balloons without airborne heaters. The restriction may be deleted when the holder of the certificate obtains the pilot experience and passes the tests required for a rating on a free balloon with an airborne heater or a gas balloon.

SUBPART E — COMMERCIAL PILOTS

61.123 Eligibility requirements: general.

To be eligible for a commercial pilot certificate, a person must—

(a) Be at least 18 years of age;

(b) Be able to speak, read, and understand English, or have an operating limitation on his pilot certificate as is necessary for safety;

(c) Hold at least a valid second-class medical certificate issued under Part 67 of this chapter, or, in the case of a glider or free balloon rating, certify that he has no known medical deficiency that makes him unable to pilot a glider or a free balloon, as appropriate;

(d) Pass a written examination appropriate to the aircraft rating sought on the subjects in which ground instruction is required by 61.125;

(e) Pass an oral and flight test appropriate to the

rating he seeks, covering items selected by the inspector or examiner from those on which training is required by 61.127; and

(f) Comply with the provisions of this subpart which apply to the rating he seeks.

61.125 Aeronautical knowledge.

An applicant for a commercial pilot certificate must have logged ground instruction from an authorized instructor, or must present evidence showing that he has satisfactorily completed a course of instruction or home study, in at least the following areas of aeronautical knowledge appropriate to the category of aircraft for which a rating is sought.

(e) *Free balloons.*

(1) The regulations of this chapter pertinent to commercial free balloon piloting privileges, limitations, and flight operations;

(2) The use of aeronautical charts and the magnetic compass for free balloon navigation;

(3) The recognition of weather conditions significant to free balloon flight operations, and the procurement and use of aeronautical weather reports and forecasts appropriate to free ballooning;

(4) Free balloon flight and ground instruction procedures; and

(5) Operating principles and procedures for free balloons, including emergency procedures such as crowd control and protection, high wind and water landings, and operations in proximity to buildings and power lines.

61.127 Flight proficiency.

The applicant for a commercial pilot certificate must have logged instruction from an authorized flight instructor in at least the following pilot opera-

tions. In addition, his logbook must contain an endorsement by an authorized flight instructor who has given him the instruction certifying that he has found the applicant prepared to perform each of those operations competently as a commercial pilot.

(f) *Free balloons.*

(1) Inflating, rigging, and mooring a free balloon;
(2) Ground and flight crew briefing;
(3) Ascents;
(4) Descents;
(5) Landings;
(6) Operation of airborne heater, if balloon is so equipped; and
(7) Emergency operations, including the use of the ripcord (may be simulated), and recovery from a terminal velocity descent if a balloon with an airborne heater is used.

61.137 Free balloon rating: aeronautical experience.

An applicant for a commercial pilot certificate with a free balloon rating must have the following flight time as pilot:

(a) If a gas balloon or a hot air balloon with an airborne heater is used, a total of at least 35 hours of flight time as pilot, including—

(1) 20 hours in free balloons; and
(2) 10 flights in free balloons, including—

(i) Six flights under the supervision of a commercial free balloon pilot;
(ii) Two solo flights;
(iii) Two flights of at least 2 hours duration if a gas balloon is used, or at least 1 hour duration if a hot air balloon with an airborne heater is used; and
(iv) One ascent under control to more than 10,000 feet above the takeoff point if a gas balloon is used or 5,000 feet above the takeoff point if a hot air balloon with an airborne heater is used.

(b) If a hot air balloon without an airborne heater is used, ten flights in free balloons, including—

(1) Six flights under the supervision of a commercial free balloon pilot; and
(2) Two solo flights.

61.139 Commercial pilot privileges and limitations: general.

The holder of a commercial pilot certificate may:

(a) Act as pilot in command of an aircraft carrying persons or property for compensation or hire;

(b) Act as pilot in command of an aircraft for compensation or hire; and

(c) Give flight instruction in an airship if he holds a lighter-than-air category and an airship class rating, or in a free balloon if he holds a free balloon class rating.

61.141 Airship and free balloon ratings: limitations.

(a) If the applicant for a free balloon class rating takes his flight test in a hot air balloon without an airborne heater, his pilot certificate contains an endorsement restricting the exercise of the privileges of that rating to hot air balloons without airborne heaters. The restriction may be deleted when the holder of the certificate obtains the pilot experience and passes the test required for a rating on a free balloon with an airborne heater or a gas balloon.

(b) If the applicant for a free balloon class rating takes his flight test in a hot air balloon with an airborne heater, his pilot certificate contains an endorsement restricting the exercise of the privileges of that rating to hot air balloons with airborne heaters. The restriction may be deleted when the holder of the certificate obtains the pilot experience required for a rating on a gas balloon.

61.193 Flight instructor authorizations.

(a) The holder of a flight instructor certificate is authorized, within the limitations of his instructor certificate and ratings, to give—

(1) In accordance with his pilot ratings, the flight instruction required by this Part for a pilot certificate or rating;

(2) Ground instruction or a home study course required by this Part for a pilot certificate and rating;

(3) Ground and flight instruction required by this subpart for a flight instructor certificate rating, if he meets the requirements prescribed in 61.187 for the issuance of a flight instructor certificate;

(4) The flight instruction required for an initial solo or cross-country flight; and

(5) The flight review required in 67.57 (a).

(b) The holder of a flight instructor certificate is authorized within the limitations of his instructor certificate to endorse—

(1) In accordance with 61.87 (d) (1) and 61.93 (c) (1), the pilot certificate of a student pilot he has instructed authorizing the student to conduct solo or solo cross-country flights, or act as pilot-in-command

of an airship requiring more than one flight crew-member.

(2) In accordance with 61.87 (d) (1), the logbook of a student pilot he has instructed authorizing single or repeated solo flights;

(3) In accordance with 61.93 (c) (2), the logbook of a student pilot whose preparation and preflight planning for a solo cross-country flight he has reviewed and found adequate for a safe flight under the conditions he has listed in the logbook;

(4) The logbook of a pilot or flight instructor he has examined certifying that the pilot or flight instructor is prepared for a written or flight test required by this Part; and

(5) In accordance with 61.187, the logbook of an applicant for a flight instructor certificate certifying that he has examined the applicant and found him competent to pass the practical test required by this Part.

(c) A flight instructor with a rotorcraft and helicopter rating or an airplane single-engine rating may also endorse the pilot certificate and logbook of a student pilot he has instructed authorizing the student to conduct solo and cross-country flights in a single-place gyroplane.

61.195 Flight instructor limitations.

The holder of a flight instructor certificate is subject to the following limitations:

(a) *Hours of instruction.* He may not conduct more than eight hours of flight instruction in any period of 24 consecutive hours.

(b) *Ratings.* He may not conduct flight instruction in any aircraft for which he does not hold a category, class, and type rating, if appropriate, on his pilot and flight instructor certificate. However, the holder of a flight instructor certificate effective on November 1, 1973 may continue to exercise the privileges of that certificate until it expires, but not later than November 1, 1975.

(c) *Endorsement of student pilot certificate.* He may not endorse a student pilot certificate for initial solo or solo cross-country flight privileges, unless he has given that student pilot flight instruction required by this Part for the endorsement, and considers that the student is prepared to conduct the flight safely with the aircraft involved.

(d) *Logbook endorsement.* He may not endorse a student pilot's logbook for solo flight unless he has

given that student flight instruction and found him prepared for solo flight in the type of aircraft involved, or for a cross-country flight, unless he has reviewed the student's flight preparation, planning, equipment, and proposed procedures and found them to be adequate for the flight proposed under existing circumstances.

(e) *Solo flights.* He may not authorize any student pilot to make a solo flight unless he possesses a valid student pilot certificate endorsed for solo in the make and model aricraft to be flown. In addition, he may not authorize any student pilot to make a solo cross-country flight unless he possesses a valid student pilot certificate endorsed for solo cross-country flight in the category of aircraft to be flown.

101.1 Applicability.

(a) This Part prescribes rules governing the operation, in the United States, of the following:

[(1) Except as provided for in 101.7 of this Part, any balloon that is moored to the surface of the earth or an object thereon and that has a diameter of more than 6 feet or a gas capacity of more than 115 cubic feet.

[(2) Except as provided for in 101.7 of this Part, any kite that weighs more than 5 pounds and is intended to be flown at the end of a rope or cable.]

(3) Any unmanned rocket except—

(i) Aerial firework displays; and

(ii) Model rockets—

(a) Using not more than 4 ounces of propellant;

(b) Using a slow-burning propellant;

(c) Made of paper, wood, or breakable plastic, containing no substantial metal parts and weighing not more than 16 ounces, including the propellant; and

(d) Operated in a manner that does not create a hazard to persons, property, or other aircraft.

[(4) Except as provided for in 101.7 of this Part, any unmanned free balloon that—]

(i) Carries a payload package that weighs more than four pounds and has a weight/size ratio of more than three ounces per square inch on any surface of the package, determined by dividing the total weight in ounces of the payload package by the area in square inches of its smallest surface;

(ii) Carries a payload package that weighs more than 6 pounds;

(iii) Carries a payload, of two or more packages, that weighs more than 12 pounds; or

(iv) Uses a rope or other device for suspension of the payload that requires an impact force of more than 50 pounds to separate the suspended payload from the balloon.

(b) For the purposes of this Part, a "gyroglider" attached to a vehicle on the surface of the earth is considered to be a kite.

101.3 Waivers.

No person may conduct operations that require a deviation from the Part except under a certificate of waiver issued by the Administrator.

101.5 Operations in prohibited or restricted areas.

No person may operate a moored balloon, kite, unmanned rocket, or unmanned free balloon in a prohibited or restricted area unless he has permission from the using or controlling agency, as appropriate.

[101.7 Hazardous operations.

[No person may operate any moored balloon, kite, unmanned rocket, or unmanned free balloon in a manner that creates a hazard to persons, property, or other aircraft.]

101.11 Applicability.

This subpart applies to the operation of moored balloons and kites. However, a person operating a moored balloon or kite within a restricted area must comply only with 101.19 and with additional limitations imposed by the using or controlling agency, as appropriate.

101.13 Operating limitations.

(a) Except as provided in paragraph (b) of this section, no person may operate a moored balloon or kite—

(1) Less than 500 feet from the base of any cloud;

(2) More than 500 feet above the surface of the earth;

(3) From an area where the ground visibility is less than three miles; or

(4) Within five miles of the boundary of any airport.

(b) Paragraph (a) of this section does not apply to the operation of a balloon or kite below the top of any structure and within 250 feet of it, if that shielded operation does not obscure any lighting on the structure.

101.15 Notice requirements.

No person may operate an unshielded moored balloon or kite more than 150 feet above the surface of the earth unless at least 24 hours before beginning the operation, he gives the following information to the FAA ATC facility that is nearest to the place of intended operation:

(a) The names and addresses of the owners and operators.

(b) The size of the balloon or the size and weight of the kite.

(c) The location of the operation.

(d) The height above the surface of the earth at which the balloon or kite is to be operated.

(e) The date, time, and duration of the operation.

101.17 Lighting and marking requirements.

(a) No person may operate a moored balloon or kite during the night unless the balloon or kite, and its mooring lines, are lighted so as to give a visual warning equal to that required for obstructions to air navigation in the FAA publication "Obstruction Marking and Lighting".

(b) No person may operate a moored balloon or kite by day unless its mooring lines have colored pennants or streamers attached at not more than 500-

foot intervals beginning at 150 feet above the surface of the earth and visible for at least one mile.

101.9 Rapid deflation device.

No person may operate a moored balloon unless it has a device that will automatically and rapidly deflate the balloon if it escapes from its moorings. If the device does not function properly, the operator shall immediately notify the nearest ATC facility of the location and time of the escape and the estimated flight path of the balloon.

101.21 Applicability.

This subpart applies to the operation of unmanned rockets. However, a person operating an unmanned rocket within a restricted area must comply only with subparagraph 101.23 (g) and with additional limitations imposed by the using or controlling agency, as appropriate.

101.23 Operating limitations.

No person may operate an unmanned rocket—
(a) In a manner that creates a collision hazard with other aricraft;
(b) In controlled airspace;
(c) Within five miles of the boundary of any airport;
(d) At any altitude where clouds or obscuring phenomena of more than five-tenths coverage prevails;
(e) At any altitude where the horizontal visibility is less than five miles;
(f) Into any cloud;
(g) Within 1,500 feet of any person or property that is not associated with the operations; or
(h) At night.

101.25 Notice requirements.

No person may operate an unmanned rocket unless, within 24 to 48 hours before beginning the operation, he give the following information to the FAA ATC facility that is nearest to the place of intended operation:
(a) The names and addresses of the operators.
(b) The number of rockets to be operated.
(c) The size and weight of each rocket.
(d) The maximum altitude to which each rocket will be operated.
(e) The location of the operation.
(f) The date, time, and duration of the operation.

(g) Any other pertinent information requested by the ATC facility.

101.31 Applicability.

This subpart applies to the operation of unmanned free balloons. However, a person operating an unmanned free balloon within a restricted area must comply only with 101.33 (d) and (e) and with any additional limitations that are imposed by the using or controlling agency, as appropriate.

101.33 Operating limitations.

No person may operate an unmanned free balloon—
(a) Unless otherwise authorized by ATC, in a control zone below 2,000 feet above the surface, or in an airport traffic area;
(b) At any altitude where there are clouds or obscuring phenomena of more than five-tenths coverage;
(c) At any altitude below 60,000 feet standard pressure altitude where the horizontal visibility is less than five miles;
(d) During the first 1,000 feet of ascent, over a congested area of a city, town or settlement or an open-air assembly of persons not associated with the operation; or
(e) In such a manner that impact of the balloon, or part thereof including its payload, with the surface creates a hazard to persons or property not associated with the operation.

101.35 Equipment and marking requirements.

(a) No person may operate an unmanned free balloon unless—
(1) It is equipped with at least two payload cutdown systems or devices that operate independently of each other;
(2) At least two methods, systems, devices, or combinations thereof, that function independently of each other are employed for terminating the flight of the balloon envelope; and
(3) The balloon envelope is equipped with a radar reflective device(s) or material that will present an echo to surface radar operating in the 200 MHz to 2700 MHz frequency range.
The operator shall activate the appropriate devices required by subparagraphs (1) and (2) of this paragraph when weather conditions are less than those prescribed for operation under this subpart, or if a malfunction or any other reason makes the further

operation hazardous to other air traffic or to persons and property on the surface.

(b) No person may operate an unmanned free balloon below 60,000 feet standard pressure altitude during the night (as corrected to the altitude of operation) unless the balloon and its attachments and payload, whether or not they become separated during the operation, are lighted so as to be visible for at least five miles.

(c) No person may operate an unmanned free balloon that is equipped with a trailing antenna that requires an impact force of more than 50 pounds to break it at any point, unless the antenna has colored pennants or streamers that are attached at not more than 50-foot intervals and that are visible for at least one mile.

(d) No person may operate during the day an unmanned free balloon that is equipped with a suspen-

sion device (other than a highly conspicuously colored open parachute) more than 50 feet long, unless the suspension device is colored in alternate bands of high conspicuity colors or has colored pennants or streamers attached which are visible for at least one mile.

101.37 Notice requirements.

(a) *Prelaunch notice.* Except as provided in paragraph (b) of this section, no person may operate an unmanned free balloon unless, within 6 to 24 hours before beginning the operation, he gives the following information to the FAA ATC facility that is nearest to the place of intended operation:

(1) The balloon identification.

(2) The estimated date and time of launching, amended as necessary to remain within plus or minus 30 minutes.

(3) The location of the launching site.

(4) The cruising altitude.

(5) The forecast trajectory and estimated time to cruising altitude or 60,000 feet standard pressure altitude, whichever is lower.

(6) The length and diameter of the balloon, length of the suspension device, weight of the payload, and length of the trailing antenna.

(7) The duration of flight.

(8) The forecast time and location of impact with the surface of the earth.

(b) For solar or cosmic disturbance investigations involving a critical time element, the information in paragraph (a) of this section shall be given within 30 minutes to 24 hours before beginning the operation.

(c) *Cancellation notice.* If the operation is canceled, the person who intended to conduct the operaton shall immediately notice the nearest FAA ATC facility.

(d) *Launch notice.* Each person operating an unmanned free balloon shall notify the nearest FAA or military ATC facility of the launch time immediately after the balloon is launched.

101.39 Balloon position reports.

(a) Each person operating an unmanned free balloon shall—

(1) Unless ATC requires otherwise, monitor the course of the balloon and record its position at least every two hours; and

(2) Forward any balloon position reports requested by ATC.

(b) One hour before beginning descent, each person operating an unmanned free balloon shall forward to the nearest FAA ATC facility the following information regarding the balloon:

(1) The current geographical position.

(2) The altitude.

(3) The forecast time of penetration of 60,000 feet standard pressure altitude (if applicable).

(4) The forecast trajectory for the balance of the flight.

(5) The forecast time and location of impact with the surface of the earth.

(c) If a balloon position report is not recorded for any two-hour period of flight, the person operating an unmanned free balloon shall immediately notify the nearest FAA ATC facility. The notice shall include the last recorded position and any revision of the forecast trajectory. The nearest FAA ATC facility shall be notified immediately when tracking of the balloon is re-established.

(d) Each person operating an unmanned free balloon shall notify the nearest FAA ATC facility when the operation is ended.

31.1 Applicability.

(a) This Part prescribes airworthiness requirements for issusing type certificates, and changes to those certificates, for manned free balloons.

(b) For the purposes of this Part—

(1) A captive gas balloon is a balloon that derives its lift from a captive lighter-than-air gas;

(2) A hot air balloon is a balloon that derives its lift from heated air;

(3) The envelope is the enclosure in which the lifting means is contained;

(4) The basket is the container, suspended beneath the envelope, for the balloon occupants;

(5) The trapeze is a harness or is a seat consisting of a horizontal bar or platform suspended beneath the envelope for the balloon occupants; and

(6) The design maximum weight is the maximum total weight of the balloon, less the lifting gas or air.

31.11 Controllability.

The applicant must show that the balloon is safe-ly controllable and maneuverable during takeoff, ascent, descent, and landing without requiring exceptional piloting skill.

31.21 Loads.

Strength requirements are specified in terms of limit loads, that are the maximum load to be expected in service, and ultimate loads, that are limit loads multiplied by prescribed factors of safety. Unless otherwise specified, all prescribed loads are limit loads.

31.23 Flight load factor.

In determining limit load, the limit flight load factor must be at least 1.4.

31.25 Factor of safety.

(a) Except as specified in paragraphs (b) and (c) of this section, the factor of safety is 1.5.

(b) A factor of safety of at least five must be used in envelope design. A reduced factor of safety of at least two may be used if it is shown that the selected factor will preclude failure due to creep or instantaneous rupture from lack of rip stoppers. The selected factor must be applied to the more critical of the maximum operating pressure or envelope stress.

(c) A factor of safety of at least five must be used in the design of all fibrous or non-metallic parts of the rigging and related attachments of the envelope to basket, trapeze, or other means provided for carrying occupants. The primary attachments of the envelope to the basket, trapeze, or other means provided for carrying occupants must be designed so that failure is extremely remote or so that any single failure will not jeopardize safety of flight.

(d) In applying factors of safety, the effect of temperature, and other operating characteristics, or both, that may affect strength of the balloon must be accounted for.

(e) For design purposes, an occupant weight of at least 170 pounds must be assumed.

31.27 Strength.

(a) The structure must be able to support limit loads without detrimental effect.

(b) The structure must be substantiated by test to be able to withstand the ultimate loads for at least three seconds without failure. For the envelope, a test of a representative part is acceptable, if the part tested is large enough to include critical seams, joints, and load attachment points and members.

(c) An ultimate free-fall drop test must be made of the basket, trapeze, or other place provided for occupants. The drop test height must be that height that results in a contact velocity at least equal to the maximum contact velocity expected in service, including emergency descent conditions. The test must be made at design maximum weight on a horizontal concrete surface, with the basket, trapeze, or other means provided for carrying occupants, striking the surface of angles of 0, 15, and 30 degrees. The weight may be distributed to simulate actual conditons. There must be no distortion or failure that is likely to cause serious injury to the occupants. In the absence of a rational analysis, a drop test height of 36 inches may be used.

31.31 General.

The suitabliity of each design detail or part that bears on safety must be established by tests or analysis.

31.33 Materials.

(a) The suitability and durability of all materials must be established on the basis of experience of tests. Materials must conform to approved specifications that will ensure that they have the strength and other properties assumed in the design data.

(b) Material strength properties must be based on enough tests of material conforming to specifications so as to establish design values on a statistical basis.

31.35 Fabrication methods.

The methods of fabrication used must produce a consistently sound structure. If a fabrication process requires close control to reach this objective, the process must be performed in accordance with an approved process specification.

31.37 Fastenings.

Only approved bolts, pins, screws, and rivets may be used in the structure. Approved locking devices or methods must be used for all these bolts, pins, and screws, unless the installation is shown to be free from vibration. Self-locking nuts may not be used on bolts that are subject to rotation in service.

31.39 Protection.

Each part of the balloon must be suitably protected against deterioration or loss of strength in service due to weathering, corrosion, or other causes.

31.41 Inspection provisions.

There must be a means to allow close examination of each part that requires repeated inspection and adjustment.

31.43 Fitting factor.

(a) A fitting factor of at least 1.15 must be used in the analysis of each fitting the strength of which is not proven by limit and ulitmate load tests in which the actual stress conditions are simulated in the fitting and surrounding structure. This factor applies to all parts of the fitting, the means of attachment, and the bearing on the members joined.

(b) Each part with an integral fitting must be treated as a fitting up to the point where the section properties become typical of the member.

(c) The fitting factor need not be used if the joint design is made in accordance with approved practices and is based on comprehensive test data.

31.45 Fuel cells.

If fuel cells are used the attachments and related supporting structure must be able to withstand, without failure, any inertia loads to which the installation may be subjected, including the drop tests prescribed in 31.27(c). For pressurized fuel systems, each element and its connecting fittings must be tested to an ultimate pressure of at least twice the maximum pressure to which the system will be subjected in normal operation. In the test, no part of the system may fail or malfunction.

31.47 Heaters.

(a) If a heater is used to provide the lifting means, the system must be designed and installed so as not to create a fire hazard.

(b) There must be shielding to protect parts adjacent to the burner flame, and the occupants, from heat effects.

(c) There must be controls, instruments, or other equipment essential to the safe control and operation of the heater. They must be shown to be able to perform their intended functions during normal and emergency operation.

(d) The heater system (including the burner unit, controls, fuel lines, fuel cells, regulators, control valves, and other related elements) must be substantiated by an endurance test of at least 50 hours. In making the test, each element of the system must be installed and tested so as to simulate the actual balloon installation. The test program must be conducted so that each 10-hour part of the test includes 7 hours at maximum heat output of the heater and 3 hours divided into at least 10 equal increments between minimum and maximum heat output ranges.

(b) Both lights must have 360° horizontal coverage and must be visible for at least two miles under clear atmospheric conditions.

(c) The white light must be located not more than 20 feet below the basket, trapeze, or other means for carrying occupants. The red light must be located not less than 7, or more than 10, feet below the white light.

(d) There must be a means to retract and store the lights.

(e) The test must also include at least three flameouts and restarts.

(f) Each element of the system must be serviceable at the end of the test.

31.49 Control systems.

(a) Each control must operate easily, smoothly, and positively enough to allow proper performance of its functions. Controls must be arranged and identified to provide for convenience of operation and to prevent the possibility of confusion and subsequent inadvertent operation.

(b) Each control system and operating device must be designed and installed in a manner that will prevent jamming, chafing, or interference from passengers, cargo, or loose objects. Precaution must be taken to prevent foreign objects from jamming the controls. The elements of the control system must have design features or must be distinctly and permanently marked to minimize the possibility of incorrect assembly that could result in malfunctioning of the control system.

(c) Each balloon using a captive gas as the lifting means must have an automatic valve or appendix that is able to release gas automatically at the rate of at least 3 percent of the total volume per minute when the balloon is at its maximum operating pressure.

(d) Each hot air balloon must have a means to allow the controlled release of hot air during flight.

(e) Each hot air balloon must have a means to indicate the maximum envelope skin temperature occurring during operation. The indicator must be readily visible to the pilot and marked to indicate the limiting safe temperature of the envelope material. If the markings are on the cover glass of the instrument, there must be provisions to maintain the correct alignment of the glass cover with the face of the dial.

31.51 Ballast.

Each captive gas balloon must have a means for the safe storage and controlled release of ballast. The ballast must consist of material that, if released during flight, is not hazardous to persons on the ground.

31.53 Drag rope.

If a drag rope is used, the end that is released overboard must be stiffened to preclude the probability of the rope becoming entangled with trees, wires, or other objects on the ground.

31.55 Deflation means.

There must be a means to allow emergency deflation of the envelope so as to allow a safe emergency landing. If a system other than a manual system is used, the reliability of the system used must be substantiated.

31.57 Rip cords.

(a) If a rip cord is used for emergency deflation, it must be designed and installed to preclude entanglement.

(b) The force required to operate the rip cord may not be less than 25, or more than 75 pounds.

(c) The end of the rip cord to be operated by the pilot must be colored red.

(d) The rip cord must be long enough to allow an increase of at least 10 percent in the vertical dimension of the envelope.

31.59 Trapeze, basket, or other means provided for occupants.

(a) The trapeze, basket, or other means provided for carrying occupants may not rotate independently of the envelope.

(b) Each projecting object of the trapeze, basket, or other means provided for carrying occupants, that could cause injury to the occupants, must be padded.

31.61 Static discharge.

Unless shown not to be necessary for safety, there must be appropriate bonding means in the design of each balloon using flammable gas as a listing means to ensure than the effects of static discharges will not create a hazard.

31.63 Safety belts.

There must be a safety belt, harness, or other restraining means for each occupant, unless the Administrator finds it unnecessary. If installed, the belt, harness, or other restraining means and its supporting structure must meet the strength requirements of Subpart C.

31.65 Position lights.

(a) If position lights are otherwise required by this chapter, there must be one steady white position light, and one flashing red position light, with an effective flash frequency of at least 40, but not more than 100, cycles per minute.

31.71 Functional and installational requirements.

Each item of equipment on a balloon must be—

(a) Designed and installed to ensure that it will perform the intended function reliably under all reasonably foreseeable operating conditons;

(b) Designed to safeguard against hazards to the balloon if it malfunctions; and

(c) Shown to function properly in the balloon.

31.81 General.

The operating limitations, normal and emergency procedures, and other pertinent information peculiar to the balloon's operating characteristics and necessary for safe operation must be provided by the manufacturer by a balloon flight manual furnished with each balloon, or by a placard or marking on the balloon that is clearly visible to the operator. The operating limitations must include the maximum certificated weight.

31.83 Conspicuity.

The exterior surface of the envelope must be of a constrasting color or colors so that it will be conspicuous during flight.

31.85 Required basic equipment.

In addition to any equipment required by this subchapter for a specific kind of operation, the following equipment is required:

(a) For all balloons:
  (1) A compass.
  (2) An altimeter.
  (3) A rate of climb indicator.
(b) For hot air balloons:
  (1) A fuel quantity guage.
  (2) An envelope temperature indicator.

Part 61 (revised) of Federal Aviation Regulations, effective November 1, 1973, establishes a new concept of pilot training and certification requirements. To provide a transition to these revised requirements, Part 61 (revised) permits the applicant, for a period of 1 year after the effective date, to meet either the previous requirements or those contained in the revised part. Since the free balloon rating on the Private Pilot Certificate lighter-than-air category is newly authorized under Part 61 (revised), the applicant for that certificate must meet only the new requirements.

This flight test guide, AC 61-62, has been prepared

by Flight Standards Service of the Federal Aviation Administration to assist the applicant and his instructor in preparing for the flight test for the Private Pilot or Commercial Pilot Certificate with a lighter-than-air category and free balloon class rating under Part 61 (revised). It contains information and guidance concerning the pilot operations, procedure, and maneuvers relevant to the flight test required for those certificates. A suggested flight test checklist is included for the convenience of those who may find such a checklist useful.

In addition to providing help to the applicant and his instructor, this guide will be useful to FAA Inspectors and designated pilot examiners in the conduct and standardization of flight tests. Persons using this guide in connection with free balloon pilot training and flight tests should also refer to the applicable *Federal Aviation Regulations, Airman's Information Manual,* pertinent advisory circulars, and training publications recommended by the Balloon Federation of America.

PILOT TRAINING AND CERTIFICATION CONCEPT

Part 61 of the Federal Aviation Regulations has been revised and upgraded to reflect the complexity of the modern aircraft as well as its operating environment. In the past, airman certification requirements could be met by training a student to pass a written test and then to demonstrate his ability to perform predetermined flight training maneuvers during a flight test. Rather than merely duplicating on the flight test the maneuvers used for training, the new training and certification concept requires that the applicant receive instruction in and demonstrate his competency in *all pilot operations* listed in pertinent sections of Part 61 (revised). A pilot operation, as used herein, is a group of related procedures and maneuvers involving skills and knowledge required to safely and efficiently function as a pilot. The specific procedures and maneuvers used to teach the pilot operations are not listed in Part 61 (revised). Instead, the instructor is permitted to select procedures and maneuvers from recognized training publications pertinent to the certificate or rating sought. The instructor indicates by logbook endorsement that the applicant has demonstrated competency in all the required pilot operations and considers him qualified to pass the flight test. On the flight test, the examiner* selects the procedures and maneuvers to be performed by the applicant to show competency in each required pilot operation.

USE OF THIS GUIDE

The pilot operations in this flight test guide, indicated by Roman numerals, are required by Part 61 (revised)—61.107 for the private pilot and 61.127 for the commercial pilot. This guide is intended only to outline appropriate pilot operations and the minimum standards for the performance of each procedure or maneuver which will be accepted by the examiner as evidence of the pilot's competency. It is not intended that the applicant be tested on every procedure or maneuver within each pilot operation, but only those considered necessary by the examiner to determine competency in each pilot operation. Procedures and maneuvers listed apply to all free balloons, except where indicated.

When, in the judgment of the examiner, certain demonstrations are impractical, competency may be determined by oral testing.

This guide contains an **Objective** for each required pilot operation. Under each pilot operation, pertinent procedures or maneuvers are listed with **Descriptions** and **Acceptable Performance Guidelines**.

1. The **Objective** states briefly the purpose of each pilot operation required on the flight test.
2. The **Description** provides information on what may be asked of the applicant regarding the selected procedure or maneuver. The procedures or maneuvers listed have been found most effective in demonstrating the objective of that particular pilot operation.
3. The **Acceptable Performance Guidelines** include the factors which will be taken into account by the examiner in deciding whether the applicant has met the objective of the pilot operation. Any procedure or action, or the lack thereof, which requires the intervention of the examiner to maintain safe flight will be disqualifying.

Emphasis will be placed on procedures, knowledge, and maneuvers which are most critical to a safe performance as a balloon pilot. During the entire

*The word "examiner" is used hereafter in this guide to denote either the Federal Aviation Administration Inspector or designated pilot examiner who conducts an official flight test.

flight test, evaluation of the applicant's performance will be based primarily on his use of good operating practices and sound judgment in avoiding critical situations. Emphasis will also be placed on necessary precautions at launch and recovery sites to avoid endangering spectators or damaging property.

The applicant will be expected to know the meaning and significance of the terms important to the balloon pilot, such as:

> Equilibrium
> Superheat
> False lift
> Never-exceed envelope temperature
> Maximum continuous envelope temperature

If the flight test is taken in a hot air free balloon equipped with an airborne heater or in a hot air free balloon without an airborne heater, the applicant's certificate will contain an endorsement restricting his pilot privileges to the type balloon used for the flight test. Part 61 (revised) outlines the procedures for removal of these restrictions.

GENERAL PROCEDURES FOR FLIGHT TESTS

The ability of an applicant for a private or commercial pilot certificate, or for an aircraft rating on the certificate, to perform the required pilot operations is based on the following:

1. Executing procedures and maneuvers within the aircraft's performance capabilities and limitations, including use of the aircraft's systems.

2. Executing emergency procedures and maneuvers appropriate to the aircraft.
3. Piloting the aircraft with smoothness and accuracy.
4. Exercising judgment.
5. Applying his aeronautical knowledge.
6. Showing that he is the master of the aircraft, with the successful outcome of a procedure or maneuver never seriously in doubt.

If the applicant fails any of the required pilot operations he fails the flight test. The examiner or the applicant may discontinue the test at any time when the failure of a required pilot operation makes the applicant ineligible for the certificate or rating sought. If the test is discontinued, the applicant is entitled to credit for only those entire pilot operations that he has successfully performed.

FLIGHT TEST PREREQUISITES

An applicant for the free balloon pilot flight test is required by revised 61.39 of the Federal Aviation Regulations to have: (1) passed the appropriate free balloon pilot written test within 24 months before the date he takes the flight test, (2) the applicable instruction and aeronautical experience prescribed for the pilot certificate he seeks, (3) a written statement certifying that he has no known medical defect that makes him unable to fly a free balloon, (4) reached at least 16 years of age for a private pilot or 18 years of age for a commercial pilot, and (5) a written statement from an appropriately certificated and rated commercial pilot certifying that he has given the applicant flight instruction in preparation for the flight test within 60 days preceding the date of application and finds him competent to pass the test and to have a satisfactory knowledge of the subject areas in which he is shown to be deficient by his FAA airman written test report.

The applicant is required by revised 61.45 to provide an airworthy balloon for the flight test.

I. RIGGING, INFLATING, AND MOORING

To determine that the applicant can competently prepare the balloon for flight, determine its airworthiness, and can follow recovery procedures after flight.

A. Layout and Recovery of Equipment

1. Description The applicant may be asked to demonstrate the procedures for the deployment and recovery of the envelope, basket, suspension lines, and burner assembly, if applicable. During these procedures, he should take precautions to prevent damage to equipment and should inspect all equipment for airworthiness. The use of a checklist is recommended.

2. Acceptable Performance Guidelines
The applicant shall demonstrate a thorough knowledge of the proper procedures for the layout and recovery of equipment. Failure to follow accepted safety precautions or failure to recognize unairworthy conditions shall be disqualifying.

B. Rigging

1. Description The applicant may be asked to demonstrate the procedures and sequence for assembling and adjusting the balloon components, installation and checking of the instrument package, and the stowage of equipment. The use of a checklist is recommended.

2. Acceptable Performance Guidelines

The applicant shall demonstrate a thorough knowledge of the proper procedures for the rigging of equipment. Failure to assure that all components are securely assembled or failure to check the safetying of the deflation device shall be disqualifying.

C. Inflation

1. Description The applicant may be asked to demonstrate the procedures for inflating the balloon to proper buoyancy. He should take proper precautions to avoid fire hazards.

2. Acceptable Performance Guidelines

The applicant shall demonstrate a thorough knowledge of the inflation procedures. He shall also be knowledgeable regarding the equipment and gases being used. Any action that creates a hazard to personnel or equipment shall be disqualifying.

D. Mooring

1. Description The applicant may be asked to demonstrate a recommended method of securing the balloon in position prior to and after flight.

2. Acceptable Performance Guidelines

The applicant shall demonstrate a thorough knowledge of proper mooring techniques, as appropriate to the balloon being used.

II. GROUND AND FLIGHT CREW BRIEFING

To determine that the applicant knows the essential duties of the ground and flight crews, and that he can competently explain, supervise, and coordinate their activities.

A. Hand Signals

1. Description The applicant may be asked to demonstrate the standard visual signals used in ballooning.

2. Acceptable Performance Guidelines

The applicant shall have a thorough knowledge of the signals used for normal and emergency balloon operations.

B. Ground Crew Duties

1. Description The applicant may be asked to select a competent ground crew, brief them on their duties, and supervise and coordinate their activities.

2. Acceptable Performance Guidelines

The applicant's performance shall be evaluated on the basis of the criteria he uses in ground crew selection and on the accuracy and completeness of his brief-

ing. Failure to competently supervise and coordinate the activities of the crew shall be disqualifying.

C. Flight Crew Duties

1. Description The applicant may be asked to select a competent flight crew, brief them on their duties, and supervise and coordinate their activities.

2. Acceptable Performance Guidelines

The applicant's performance shall be evaluated on the basis of the criteria he uses in flight crew selection and on the accuracy and completeness of his briefing. Failure to competently supervise and coordinate the activities of the crew shall be disqualifying.

III. ASCENTS

To determine that the applicant can accomplish

VISUAL
WIND VELOCITY: DETERMINATION

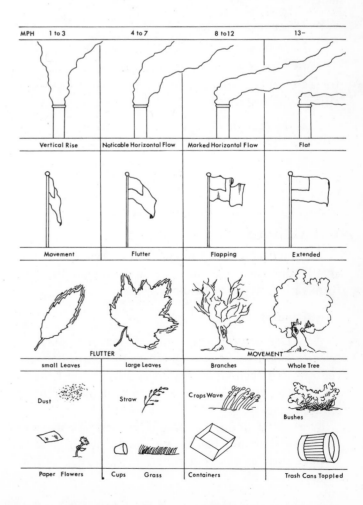

an ascent to a preselected height and can maintain that height.

A. Ascents

1. Description The applicant may be asked to demonstrate the proper procedures and techniques for a weigh-off, and for an ascent at an acceptable rate to the height specified by the examiner. In addition, he may be asked to explain the techniques and precautions to be used in various atmospheric and launch-site conditions.

2. Acceptable Performance Guidelines The applicant's performance shall be evaluated on his knowledge and use of procedures and techniques for accomplishing the weigh-off, ascent, level-off, and maintenance of altitude. Any action that creates a hazard to personnel or equipment shall be disqualifying.

IV. DESCENTS

To determine that the applicant can accomplish a descent to a preselected height and can maintain that height.

A. Descents

1. Description The applicant may be asked to demonstrate the proper procedures and techniques for a descent at an acceptable rate to the height specified by the examiner.

2. Acceptable Performance Guidelines The applicant's performance shall be evaluated on his knowledge and use of procedures and techniques for accomplishing the descent, level-off, and maintenance of altitude. Any action that creates a hazard to personnel or equipment shall be disqualifying.

V. LANDINGS

To determine that the applicant can select a suitable landing site and can safely and competently perform various types of landings.

A. Landings

1. Description The applicant may be asked to select a landing site and demonstrate the proper procedures and techniques for an approach and landing at that site. He may also be asked to demonstrate an aborted landing.

In a gas balloon, he should properly coordinate the use of gas and ballast, he should use all landing devices such as the trail rope and rip panel, as necessary.

In a hot air balloon with an airborne heater, he should demonstrate the proper use of the heater. He should also demonstrate the use of all landing devices such as the trail rope, maneuvering vent, and deflation port, if the balloon is so equipped.

2. Acceptable Performance Guidelines The applicant's performance shall be evaluated on his knowledge and use of procedures, techniques, and all landing devices for accomplishing a safe landing at the selected site. Any action that creates a hazard to personnel or equipment shall be disqualifying.

VI. OPERATION OF AIRBORN HEATER (Hot Air Balloon)

To determine that the applicant can start and operate the balloon's airborne heater in a safe and efficient manner both on the ground and in flight.

A. Ground Operation of Heater

1. Description The applicant may be asked to demonstrate the procedures for checking the heater system for fuel quantity, leaks, proper ignition, operation, and adjustments.

2. Acceptable Performance Guidelines The applicant shall be evaluated on his ability to properly perform the necessary ground checks for the heater. Any action that creates a hazard to personnel or equipment shall be disqualifying.

B. Inflight Operation of Heater

1. Description The applicant may be asked to demonstrate the proper inflight heater procedures and techniques for controlling the balloon in ascents, level flight, descents, and landings.

2. Acceptable Performance Guidelines

The applicant's performance shall be evaluated on his ability to accurately ascend, maintain level flight, descend, and land, as requested by the examiner.

VII. EMERGENCY OPERATIONS

To determine that the applicant can react promptly and correctly to emergencies which may occur during flight.

A. Emergency Use of Ripcord

1. Description The applicant may be asked to demonstrate a knowledge of the use of the ripcord in an emergency situation involving obstacles or a high-wind condition.

2. Acceptable Performance Guidelines
The applicant shall be evaluated on his knowledge of procedures, his judgment, and his timely use of the ripcord.

B. Terminal Velocity Descent (Hot Air Balloon with Airborne Heater)

1. Description The applicant may be asked to demonstrate that he can recognize a terminal velocity descent, check the descent with the heater, and recover with a minimum loss of altitude.

2. Acceptable Performance Guidelines
The applicant's performance shall be evaluated on the basis of his prompt recognition of the terminal velocity descent and his use of the heater to check the descent. Allowing the envelope temperature to exceed the maximum allowable or never-exceed temperature shall be disqualifying

C. Heater Malfunctions (Hot Air Balloon with Airborne Heater)

1. Description The applicant may be asked to demonstrate his knowledge of corrective actions for heater malfunctions such as fuel starvation, fuel flow obstructions, loss of pilot light, or jammed regulators.

2. Acceptable Performance Guidelines
The applicant shall correctly analyze heater difficulties and take proper action. Failure to have a striker-igniter, or other acceptable means for relighting the heater, aboard the aircraft shall be disqualifying.